Christ and the Chocolaterie

A Lent Course

HILARY BRAND

DARTON · LONGMAN + TODD

First published in 2002 by
Darton, Longman and Todd Ltd
1 Spencer Court
140–142 Wandsworth High Street
London SW18 4JJ

Reprinted 2003, 2006, 2009, 2012, 2013, 2015

ISBN 10: 0–232–52457–2
ISBN 13: 978–0–232–52457–4

A catalogue record for this book is available
from the British Library.

Designed by Sandie Boccacci
Phototypeset 9.5/11.5pt Times by Intype London Ltd
Printed and bound by Imak Ofset, Turkey

Contents

Introduction to the Course

The power of a story

Some people don't think that fiction can teach us anything. 'But it isn't *true*,' they say.

What they mean is that it is not factual. But just because something is not factual does not mean it doesn't have truths to teach us. In fact, very often it is just the reverse.

Suppose you were asked to write a history of your church. You would not find it difficult to write the facts: number in the congregation, the different activities, names of leaders, etc. You probably wouldn't find it too difficult to write the good things: we've had an Alpha course, we've built a new church hall, we take our kids away to camp. But quite probably, and quite rightly, you would find it hard to be totally honest. What about the difficult things – the tensions between the vicar and the organist, the time Mrs Farquarson got offended and walked out, the youth leader who left his wife for a fling with Brown Owl?

If you were writing fiction, however, you could explore these things – you could examine how the youth leader ached for some human warmth, what there was in Mrs Farquarson's childhood that made her so difficult, how the vicar went home at night and wept with frustration at trying to keep everyone happy. It might well be a far truer account of how things really are in your church, than the safe but accurate history that doesn't hurt anyone.

'But come on,' some others will say, 'surely you can't use a film like *Chocolat* as the basis for a Lent course?

This is Hollywood – this is nothing like real life'. And no, in some ways it isn't – rootless travellers rarely return to settle down (and are rarely quite as charming as Juliette Binoche and Johnny Depp), kleptomaniacs are rarely cured as quickly as Josephine Muscat, people rarely make friends with their enemies as quickly as the Comte does with Vianne. We must allow the silver screen its exaggerations and neatly knotted loose ends – we are, after all encroaching on the world of myths and legends. But then myths and legends too have a great deal to teach us.

It was Aristotle who first defined the value of their role – one he described as 'catharsis', a word that means literally a purification or purging. What Aristotle meant was that by identifying with the drama, the audience is provided with a safe place to draw out and examine buried feelings – anger, fear, pain, lust – which exploding into another context could be dangerous. A screenwriter acquaintance of mine describes his work as follows: 'I want to make people feel so much that they start to think.'

Many films are great starting points for exploring big issues about God, the world and what it means to be human. If this course does nothing more than introduce a few more people to the depths that even a fairly light and frivolous film can plumb, then it will have done its job.

The strength of an image

Films, like the Bible, are crammed full of visual metaphors. Often, as in the Bible, they use elemental images – sun, rain, fire, wind, grain, wine – to 'speak' of some abstract concept – blessing, testing, passion, change, strength, joy – in a deeper way than words ever could. Occasionally a film thrusts these images at you so that you cannot miss them. But often it does not – mostly they are fleeting and seemingly accidental. They never are – when it costs tens of thousands of dollars for even a few seconds of film footage, you can be certain that absolutely everything you see and hear is completely intentional. You may not consciously 'read' these images at all, and the director knows you will not, but subconsciously they will do their work.

So as you view *Chocolat* (and, in order to pursue this course, it is essential to have seen the film in full before you start), you may find it interesting and instructive to look out for these sorts of images and sounds as the film progresses. Why are they there? What are they saying?

The depth of a character

At a screenwriting class I attended (it has so far born no celluloid fruit, but was fascinating none the less), I was told that when I created my characters, I needed to 'Know them as well as God knows them.' Good screenwriters will work out a complete biography of each of the film's major characters: what their childhood was like, what their formative experiences were, what it is deep down that drives them. They will know what it was like for the Comte to grow up learning of his illustrious forebears and being told that he had to follow their example. They will know how Anouk felt in the school playgrounds of Vienna and Andalucia. Sometimes this information never even appears in the film. But often it does – often there are little clues as to where this person is coming from and what it is that makes them behave the way they do. Look out for these little pointers too, as you view *Chocolat*. They will throw light on the character's actions and by doing so may even throw light on your own!

The benefit of a repeat viewing

You will see even from the examples I have given above, that there is far more in any film than you are likely to absorb in one sitting. This course allows for one full viewing of the film, plus excerpts during each session. However, if you can find time to view the film for yourself a second or even third time, you will probably find it rewarding. For group leaders, I would suggest that a second full viewing is almost essential. However, in case your memory needs jogging, following is a list of the main characters:

Vianne	the journeying chocolate maker, daughter of Chitza and George
Anouk	her daughter
Comte de Reynaud	the Mayor of Lasquenet
Roux	the 'river rat'
Armande Voisin	old lady with diabetes, Caroline's mother
Caroline Clairmont	daughter to Armande, mother to Luc, secretary to the Comte
Serge Muscat	drunken cafe owner
Josephine Muscat	his battered wife
Guillaume Blerot	retired gentleman with dog Charlie
Madame Audel	widow to whom Guillaume is attracted
Père Henri	priest
Yvette Marceau	sex-starved wife
Alphonse Marceau	weary husband

The need for a safe environment

When I was talking of the value of film earlier, I spoke of 'catharsis' and the value of a safe environment in which to allow deep issues to surface. In taking this film out of the darkened cinema or the privacy of your sitting room, and examining it in depth, are we therefore making it unsafe?

I have been to an awful lot of Christian meetings that were heavy on 'cringe factor'. Do you know the sort of thing? The 'Turn to the person next to you and tell them how God has blessed you' syndrome. I have cringed frequently enough not to wish to impose it on you here. I know that you may not wish to bare your soul to a stranger, and even less to an acquaintance whom you greet occasionally at the church door or in the post office. But I also know that churches at their best are real communities where people can relate to each other at an honest and accepting level. After all, if we can't do it here, where we know that God loves us, complete with all our baggage and failings, then where can we do it?

I have tried here, therefore, to create a course where there is freedom to speak honestly, but not compulsion to do so if you don't feel comfortable with it. But be brave – almost always if you speak out something hard to share, you will find it will immediately create echoes in the hearts of your hearers.

But being a hearer of someone else's honest words puts a responsibility on you:

- Firstly, *confidentiality*. It cannot be a safe environment if the speaker fears that what he or she says will be repeated and dissected elsewhere.
- Secondly, *respect*. Even though you feel you may have great wisdom on a subject, never descend on someone with advice and pat answers. Resist the urge to tell anyone in the group that they are wrong. Questions, maybe – condemnatory statements never. Watch the film, incidentally, to see how Vianne tackles this sort of situation.
- Last but not least, *genuine listening* is often the greatest gift you can offer someone. Give each speaker your whole attention. Resist the urge to think about what you want to say next. Let other people's words sink in rather than float over you and you will be enriched by the experience.

The meaning of community

The word 'community' is often used to describe a group of people who just happen to be thrown together by geography or a common interest. True community, however, is far deeper – and quite rare. The following definition, based on the writings of Dr M. Scott Peck, seems to me to encapsulate what the film *Chocolat* and what this course is about: 'We define community as a group of people who, regardless of their backgrounds and beliefs, have been able to accept and transcend their differences, enabling them to communicate effectively and openly.' I hope that as your group embarks on this Lenten journey, it will enable you too to become community to each other.

The blessings and barbs of the Book

The book I am referring to is not the book on which the film is based (see below), but the Bible. You will find that each week's section includes a passage for you to read individually to introduce the topic, and one to follow up your thinking afterwards. And each of these includes a Bible passage (almost entirely about the things that Jesus did or said).

Now I know from experience, not least my own, that the one thing most people don't get round to doing is actually opening the Bible and reading the passages for themselves. Yes, I can imagine how busy you are, and I expect many of you may be familiar with the passages, and I've often skipped the Bible bit too, but I implore you – just now and then, do make time to open the Book and read the Gospel and give yourself a bit of space to mull it over. It may, at first glance, seem simple and familiar. It may contain some hard sayings. It may raise more questions than answers. But I'd be prepared to bet on it – read the Bible reflectively and nine times out of ten you will be surprised by the result.

Postscript – book versus film

Many people may have read the original book of *Chocolat*. I'm sorry to disappoint you if the book is a favourite, but this course completely ignores it. This is not because it is not a good book. It is simply because book and film are quite different. In the book, for instance, the character of the Comte is the local priest. The book is set in the present day and the film in the late 1950s. Some characters in the book are compacted into one in the film. Oh, and the endings are different. So to avoid confusion, this course focuses entirely on the film.

Week One:
Giving Up – The Prelude to Change

I love chocolate – dark and bitter, rich and creamy, lemon creams, mint thins, caramels, truffles, pralines, profiteroles, Mars bars, Mississippi mud pies – even the names make my mouth water. I'm a fruit and nut case, I've had more Yorkies than one of Eddie Stobart's drivers, I would definitely not give you my last Rolo.

I also weigh 13 stone.

I am appalled to see this statement in print, but I screwed up my courage and put it here for a good reason. I want to make an honest admission that, where food is concerned, I am very bad indeed at giving up. Or, put another way, where diets and exercise are concerned, I am very good at giving up.

I am telling you this to explain that, wonderful as chocolate is, for me it can quite genuinely become an addiction. I know that food is the first thing I turn to when I am stressed, and that the wrong sort of food makes me sluggish and slobbish and a lookalike for Jabba the Hutt's auntie. I am all too aware that because there is more of me than there ought to be, in other aspects there is less of me than there could be. I know that when I do eat less and exercise more, I have more energy to put into my life. I know that unless I shed a few stone, I will never be able to see the sunrise from the top of Mount Sinai, wear the latest fashions or dance without feeling silly – all things I would love to do.

I begin this way to show you one reason at least why

Chocolat's seductive celebration of 'if it feels good do it' may need to be looked at with something of a critical eye. (Another, of course, is the fact that much of the chocolate we eat in the West is produced in the Third World in conditions of near slavery – see p. 82, 'The Unfair Economics of Chocolate'.)

The film's philosophy of indulging yourself, enjoying life and learning to be yourself very much taps into the spirit of our age. Now, there are some very healthy aspects to all of those attitudes, and the last thing I want to be is a Comte (or Grinch or Scrooge). All the same, my knowledge of the Christian faith leads me to wonder whether we should jettison self-denial that easily. It is all too easy to take on the 'feel-good' message of a film without thinking. Perhaps we should first explore whether the idea of 'giving something up for Lent' – be it chocolate, wine, television or sex – is a valid one? Is it even a Christian one?

Origins of Lent

The name 'Lent' comes from the Saxon word *Lenctentid*, used for the month of March and signifying springtide and the lengthening of days. The idea of a fast before Easter, however, goes back way before Christianity reached the Saxons, to the first centuries of the Church. It seems to have sprung up spontaneously, albeit only originally practised for two or three days before Easter. The earliest known reference to a forty-day fast was in 325 CE as one of the 'canons' (church rules) arising from the Council of Nicaea, where church leaders from all of the then Christian world met to thrash out a mutual understanding of what they believed. It became common practice that for forty days only one meal a day was eaten, with no meat or fish. (As to whether chocolate was allowed, see p. 77, 'The Curious History of Chocolate'.)

The forty days, of course, is an echo of Christ's time of

fasting in the wilderness. But Christ never commanded his followers to fast (although he did assume it as a common practice, talking in Matthew 6:16 about 'when you fast', rather than 'if'), and neither did the apostles. So why did the practice arise? The main reason seems to be that baptisms at that time only happened once a year, at Easter. Lent was instituted as a preparation for baptism – public entry to the Christian faith – and for those who wanted to renew their baptismal vows.

Christ's fast in the wilderness had a purpose – it was as a prelude to a major change in his life: the beginning of a ministry that would change the face of history. When he called his followers to give up anything, that too was in order to set them free to follow a new direction.

It was in order that they might be radically changed – and that their change would change their world. So it was in the first centuries of Christendom – Lent was a time of preparation for a major life change.

Read Matthew 4:1–11, 18–22

Pause for thought

NB: This is an exercise in imagination – there are no right or wrong answers.
*What would have happened if Jesus had **not** withdrawn to the desert and been tempted for forty days before he began his ministry?*
*What would have happened if Peter and Andrew, James and John had **not** given up the security of their employment and followed Jesus?*

And a further pause

As well as pondering the above, if you can possibly find the time, please read the following passage, and reflect on the following question. Both questions will be discussed during the group evening.

Read Mark 10:17-27

What would have happened if the rich young man had given away everything that he owned and embarked on a new life? What might have happened to him if he had not?

GROUP SESSION

Show video   **5 min.**
Chocolate beans awakening weary husband's passion for loo-scrubbing wife; Comte in study refusing food; Josephine going into chocolaterie; Guillaume meeting three widows.

Discuss   **20–30 min.**
Either all together or divide into groups and allocate one or two questions to each group. (If divided into groups then use 10–20 minutes in groups and 10 minutes for report back.)

1. What motivates the Comte to his frugal diet? Is it his own physical, mental or physical health? If not, then what is it?
2. Many people 'give up' aspects of their lives without ever intending to do so. Think about the characters in that film clip – what have they 'given up' *unintentionally*?
3. If a stranger turned up in your church, what things that they saw or heard might make them think that Christianity is more about what you don't do, than what you do?

(Possible supplementary question if needed)

4. Have any of you used Lent as a period of self-denial? If so, then what motivated you to do so? If you are not familiar with the idea of Lenten self-denial, how does it strike you?

Brainstorm   **10–15 min.**

A chance for everyone to chip in with as many quick-fire answers as possible. Elect someone as scribe to write up answers and display them if possible on a board or pinned-up sheet of paper.

5. Make a list of all the things you can think of that it might be beneficial to give up – whether for a short while, a long while or for ever.
6. List all the reasons you can think of *why* giving up any of those things might be beneficial.
7. Highlight all items on the list that are beneficial, or at least harmless, if taken in moderation.

Show video   **5 min.**

Comte taking Serge to confession; catechism class; time passing; villagers in confessional; Comte at home drinking water with lemon.

As you watch, notice what short scene comes just before the sequence where the villagers are making their confession.

Discuss   **5–10 min.**

8. *Chocolat* is superficially about a battle between giving up food and enjoying chocolate. But what other behavioural changes of the 'if it feels good, do it' variety does the film explore?
   Clue A: What was the image on screen immediately before the confessional sequence? No scene in a film is ever there by accident. What was the director trying

to say by putting this just before a sequence of people confessing their indulgence and lack of self-control? **Clue B:** When is the film set? What is significant about this period in social history?

9. In your opinion, is Vianne a brave freedom fighter or a sinister and subversive destroyer of traditional values?

Imagine 10–15 min.

This is an exercise in imagination – there is no 'right answer' to these questions. Hopefully, group members will have read the stories and thought about the questions for themselves beforehand. If this has not happened, then the group leader may need to give an explanatory introduction to each Gospel incident.

10. What would have happened if Jesus had *not* withdrawn to the desert and been tempted for forty days before he began his ministry?

What would have happened if Peter and Andrew, James and John had *not* given up the security of their employment and followed Jesus?

11. What could have happened if the rich young man *had* given away everything that he owned and embarked on a new life? What might have happened to him if he did *not*?

Meditation 10–15 min.

Silence *(3–5 min.)*

In the silence, ask God to show you:

• anything it might be healthy – mentally, physically or spiritually – for you to give up;

• anything you have inadvertently given up that it might be time for you to rediscover.

Reader 1: Some words of ancient wisdom from Ecclesiastes 3:1–8: 'To everything there is a season . . .'

Pause

Reader 2: Some words of St Paul, grappling with the ethical issues of his day, from 1 Corinthians 6:12 and 19–20: 'Everything is permissible, but . . .'

Silence (*3–5 min.*)

Reader 3: Prayer
Father God, who created all things for our delight, help us to live life to the full. Teach us never to neglect or refuse the many good things you offer us. Teach us to appreciate the simple joys of being human, and teach us, in our turn, to create delight for others.

But, Lord, keep us alert, lest we start to use your good gifts in a way that you never intended. Keep us from the over-indulgence that turns healthy appetite into addiction. Teach us that fruit out of season can be sweet to the lips yet poison to the body. Strengthen our weak wills and deal with those deep longings that make us crave what is bad for us.

We ask, Lord, for your forgiveness when we fail . . . we acknowledge that it is 'when' and not 'if', because each of us is fallible. We ask you that, because of this fallibility we all share, you will help us to be gentle with ourselves and with others . . . as you are with us.

In the name of the demanding, forgiving, probing and gentle Christ. Amen.

Silence (*optional*) (*1 min.*)

TO CONTINUE YOUR THINKING
(Read this after the meeting)

It is fascinating to note that fasting is a common factor in all major religions and even among those with no religion – as the proprietors of health farms and Weight Watchers can testify. Perhaps what we are looking at is a common human urge to strip life back now and again to the basics. Perhaps it is an instinctive feeling that in order to be more spiritually aware, there are times when the material things you so depend on just have to go.

Giving up is, of course, not just about a healthy body. There are ways in which mind and spirit can be honed and strengthened by times of abstinence, not least from the constant pressures and distractions of our frenetic world. Perhaps this is the New Age movement's gift to the Church – to remind us that our well-being is a holistic issue: body, mind and spirit.

There may come a point, though, where New Age philosophy parts company with the New Testament. For Christ's message is inescapable – self-denial is not only about the good it does to *me*.

In this course, we are exploring not only 'giving up' but also 'giving out'.

If you want to give to others, it will almost always involve giving up something you would rather keep for yourself. Nursing a sick relative involves a loss of time and freedom. Making a donation to Oxfam involves not spending on something you might otherwise afford. And there are some evils that simply cannot be conquered at a distance. There are times when someone must be willing to give up creature comforts and security and just go.

Chocolat could easily be seen as an anti-Lent film, but then again, Vianne could easily be seen as a role model of the sort of self-denial Christ advocated – going without security and status in order to fulfil a calling as a kind of travelling healer. It is a calling with a cost, to Vianne and to her daughter, and like all callings, it raises hard questions. Am I really doing this because I am called, or because I am driven? How far is it right to impose my calling on my child?

'Count the cost,' says Jesus, to those who want to build something in their lives. 'No pain, no gain,' say today's fitness instructors.

Another confession (not quite so terrible, since I imagine almost everyone reading this book could say the same) – I have lived very comfortably for pretty well all of my life. I am used to hot water, central heating and a decent mattress, and have no desire to forgo them. I have not yet been a missionary, or an aid worker. Somehow these particular tasks have never come my way. But I said 'not yet' because I would like to think that if God ever needs me – be it feeding refugees, visiting old ladies, or campaigning for change; be it in the Third World, the inner city, or even a French village – I am not so addicted to security, routine and comfort that I would be unable to meet the challenge.

I would like to think so, but . . .

Am I so physically, mentally and spiritually flabby that I am likely to miss the opportunities that God wants to give me? To be honest, I don't know.

Do you?

Read Luke 5:27–32; 7:36–50

Jesus did not prepare himself for ministry in order to make himself some sort of super-spiritual being. He prepared himself for a life among people, all sorts of people. Being where they were, doing what they did. Listening, talking, healing, challenging, risk-taking, absorbing all the criticisms thrown at him.

'Giving up' is of limited value if it does not result in 'giving out'.

Pause for thought

Again this is an exercise in imagination – no right or
wrong answers.

*What might have been different, both at the time and in
the centuries that followed, if Jesus had refused to attend the
tax collector's party or the Pharisee's dinner?*

Week Two:
Giving Out – The Power of a Gift

TO START YOU THINKING

Pause for thought

Try and remember times when others have done something or said something that has made you feel loved and accepted.

The gift of encouragement

I am frequently surprised by things that other people remember that I have forgotten completely.

'Do you remember,' said my very oldest friend recently, 'when I was eleven you and some of the others bought me a pencil case for my birthday? It was the first time anyone except my immediate family had bought me a present and it meant such a lot.'

'I always remember,' said another friend, 'when you organised a party for my twenty-first birthday.'

A letter arrived a few months ago. It was from the minister of a church we once attended, someone I hadn't seen for twenty years or so, who had just read an article I had written. 'I still remember your kindness,' he said, 'in travelling all the way to see us in our new church.'

All these things I had forgotten. I am not writing them now to tell you what a nice person I am – rather the opposite. I think God may have sent these little reminders to tell me something else I was in danger of forgetting – that little kindnesses may be far more important in the scheme of things than running an efficient office or writing successful books.

There are certain other things I remember though, that the person who did them has probably long since forgotten.

The encouraging words spoken by another student on a writing course, when I had just nervously shared my first attempts at fiction and was feeling completely out of my depth. The girl at my new job, whom I hardly knew but who bothered to say, 'I like your outfit. You always wear nice clothes.' I'm not sure it was true, but it made me feel so much better.

The card that arrived one day months after we had moved to a new area, from an old friend just to say she missed us. It didn't matter that it was so late, God arranged it that it came at just the right time when we needed encouragement.

Some other things that frequently take me by surprise:

- The number of times someone who at first glance I thought might be boring or 'not my type' turns out to be someone whose company I enjoy.
- The number of times I think I am doing a good turn for someone, only to find that the benefits I receive back far outweigh what I gave.
- The number of times getting to know someone from another country, another culture or another belief system has enriched me.

The gift of acceptance

Read Luke 14:1–24

This parable is often taken to refer to the Jews and Gentiles: God had invited the Jews to become part of his kingdom and too often they had refused, so now he was opening it up to the Gentiles. While that may be true,

Jesus' forthright comment in verses 12–14 shows that he was not just trying to make a religious point. He meant it quite – shockingly – literally.

Pause for thought

What could you say to encourage someone today? How could you show acceptance this week to someone who feels unaccepted?

GROUP SESSION

Show video 10 min.
Armande reminiscing; Vianne's gift to Josephine; Vianne visiting Josephine.

Brainstorm 10 min.
In a quick-fire session, think of as many answers to the following questions as you can, and elect someone as scribe to write them up on a board or large sheet of paper.

1. For the moment, leave aside any questions you may have about Vianne, her pagan influences, her motives, etc., and look just at the good things she does. In this clip, how does she reach out to other people? List all the different things she does and says in this clip that offer people love and acceptance.

2. Cast your mind back to when Vianne first met both Armande and Josephine. How did they behave? List the things they said and did which might well have put her off getting to know them. How would you have reacted to those initial encounters?

3. Hopefully (!) your church has plenty of people who are prickly, difficult, a bit odd or socially unaccept-

able. List all the reactions in you which might make you back off from them.

Readings 3–5 min.
Reader 1: Luke 5:27–32

Pause (*optional*) (*1 min.*)

Reader 2: Luke 7:36–50

Pause (*optional*) (*1 min.*)

Ponder and share 10–20 min.
Take 3–5 minutes' silence to think about the following questions. Afterwards, if you feel you want to, share your thoughts with the group. You may prefer to divide into small groups for this.

4. Think about ways in which someone's act of generosity to you – whether of time, respect, listening, a practical gift, showing appreciation for what you had to offer them, etc. – has made a difference to your life.

5. Are there any people that you first felt uncomfortable with or disliked, who have turned out to enrich your life?

Show video 5 min.
Armande's party.

Discuss 5–10 min.
6. Vianne arranged the party for Armande knowing that the rich food, especially sweet things, could kill her. In the circumstances, was it a right thing to do? To what extent should we give people what they want, even if we know it is bad for them?

Ponder and share   10–20 min.

One of the greatest gifts we can give to others is our time. And often, what they need most is not counsel or prayer or deep conversation but just time spent having fun. One of the most neglected gifts is the gift of an invitation – to a meal, a walk, a cup of tea, a cinema trip – it need not be anything grand or elaborate.

Spend a few minutes in silence to think about the following questions before sharing your thoughts. Again this may best be done in a small group.

7. Think of a time when an invitation came as a special gift to you.

8. Do you spend enough time having fun with others? When was the last time you had a good laugh? Does your church community as a whole spend enough time together doing social things (whether formal organised activities or informal ones)?

9. What are the reasons you give for not spending more time having fun with others?
   - The business of living – earning money, looking after the family, doing up the house – takes up all my time.
   - A Christian's mission and purpose is too important to allow time for fun.
   - Don't have anyone to do it with.

10. What are the actual reasons?
   - Too tired to bother.
   - Not confident in arranging anything.
   - Scared of being rebutted if I invite anyone.
   - Other?

Meditation   10 min.

Silence

Reader 3:
Friendship is a fragile thing and must be approached gently and patiently. The following passage explores this idea. It is taken from *The Little Prince*, a fantasy story by Antoine de Saint-Exupéry about a boy who lives alone on a tiny planet with a rose bush as his only companion. The boy journeys to find other worlds, and on another such tiny planet he meets a fox:

"Come and play with me," proposed the little prince, "I am so unhappy."

"I cannot play with you," the fox said, "I am not tamed." . . .

"What does that mean – 'tame'?"

"It is an act too often neglected," said the fox. "It means to establish ties."

" 'To establish ties'?"

"Just that," said the fox. "To me you are still nothing more than a little boy who is just like a hundred thousand other little boys. And I have no need of you. And you, on your part, have no need of me. To you I am nothing more than a fox like a hundred thousand other foxes. But if you tame me, then we shall need each other. To me you will be unique in all the world. To you, I shall be unique in all the world."

"I am beginning to understand," said the little prince. "There is a flower. I think she has tamed me." . . .

"One only understands the things that one tames," said the fox. "Men have no more time to understand anything. They buy things already made at the shops. But there is no shop anywhere where you can buy friendship, and so men have no friends any more. If you want a friend, tame me."

"What must I do to tame you?" asked the little prince.

"You must be very patient," replied the fox. "First

you will sit down a little distance from me – like that –
in the grass. I shall look at you out of the corner of
my eye and you will say nothing. Words are a source
of misunderstandings. But you will sit a little closer
to me every day . . ."

And so the little prince does, and eventually he and the
fox become friends. Later the fox explains more:

"It is the time you wasted for your rose that makes
your rose so important . . . Men have forgotten this
truth," said the fox. "But you must not forget it. You
become responsible for what you have tamed. You are
responsible for your rose . . ."

Silence *(30 sec.–1 min.)*

Reader 4:
A well-known passage from Paul's letter to the Corinthians – so well known that the radical nature of its
message may have lost the power to shock us:
1 Corinthians 13:1–10.

Silence *(30 sec.–1 min.)*

Reader 5:
A prayer using the words of a song:

Teach me to dance
    to the beat of your heart,
Teach me to move
    in the power of your Spirit,
Teach me to walk
    in the light of your presence,
Teach me to dance
    to the beat of your heart.

Teach me to love
    with your heart of compassion,

Teach me to trust
    in the word of your promise,
Teach me to hope
    in the day of your coming,
Teach me to dance
    to the beat of your heart.
               Amen.

Silence (*optional*)   (*1 min.*)

TO CONTINUE YOUR THINKING

The gift of hospitality

One thing that disappoints me about the Gospels is that Jesus never gave a party (except perhaps the Last Supper, which was understandably somewhat sombre in tone).

But even if he never gave one, he was a welcome guest at several, spoke of others, and never showed any hint of disapproval no matter how disreputable the company. His followers certainly made it clear that welcoming others into your home was an important factor of this new religion.

'Practise hospitality,' says Paul succinctly to the Roman church (Romans 12:13).

'Offer hospitality to one another without grumbling,' writes Peter (1 Peter 4:9).

The first Christians, according to their chronicler Luke, 'broke bread in their homes and ate together with glad and sincere hearts' (Acts 2:46).

In a way, Christianity did not need to say a great deal about hospitality. When Moses formulated the Jewish religion by listening to God and recording what he heard, periods of feasting and celebration were set in place as a vital part of the cycle of life.

And of course, entertaining strangers was so ingrained

into the Jewish way of life – indeed of all Middle Eastern life, as it is today – that the writer to the Hebrews needed only to remind them: 'Do not forget to entertain strangers, for by so doing some people have entertained angels without knowing it' (Hebrews 13:2). The story of Abraham, who found that the travellers he had invited into his tent were actually messengers from God, was so well known as not to need naming.

But of the many good things that have transferred from biblical times into Western Christianity, sadly, hospitality is not always one of them. It almost seems that the more we have the less willing we are to share it.

Pause for thought

What do you think are the reasons why you and those you know are sometimes reluctant to invite others into your homes?

Read John 2:1–11

I often wonder how the staunch Temperance supporters of previous centuries managed to explain this one. Jesus' first miracle, and he uses it for something as frivolous as providing wine for a party. And not just for the toasts either. Verse 10 suggests that the celebrations were already fairly far gone by the time this occurred. Do you think Jesus did this to make a statement, or just to give help where it was needed? Whether it was an intentional statement or not, what messages does this story send to you?

Pause for thought

What act of hospitality could you perform in the next few weeks? It need not be anything grand – the aim is to make someone feel loved and accepted, not to impress them.

Week Three:
Getting Wise – The Possibility of Change

TO START YOU THINKING

Pause for thought

What answer would you give to the question, what is the film Chocolat *about? Take a few minutes to think about it before reading on.*

One thing that has fascinated me as I have discussed this film is the variety of answers I have heard to the above question. *It's about Lent versus chocolate. It's about self-denial versus self-indulgence. It's about traditional religion versus alternative therapies/beliefs. It's about tolerance and welcoming strangers. It's about what you do being more important than what you don't do.* Yes, it is all these things and more, and they will all come up during this course. But I want to turn now to something you may not have thought of. Because I think that at its heart this film is about *control.*

The imaginary French town of Lasquenet is like most communities, especially religious ones – it works as an unspoken pact between those who control and those who assent to be controlled. It is ruled by habits (be it Lent, mistrust of the 'river rats' or the Widow Audel's protracted mourning) whose original reasons have been lost in the mists of time. The arrival of Vianne, the stranger who refuses to accept their norms, throws everything into confusion.

Read Matthew 12:1–21

So it was in first-century Palestine, only this time the uncomfortable stranger was Jesus, striding across the Judean countryside, ignoring petty restrictions, turning the tables, showing no fear for those who dominated or controlled.

Strange, then, that the Church that bears his name is so often known as the most traditional, hierarchical and authoritarian institution around. Strange but true – there is no shortage of evidence to bear this out.

Playwright Edward Bond, writing in the 1960s, claimed that 'God is a secular mechanism, a device of class rule.' Before you dismiss that as left-wing, 'angry young man' rhetoric, look at his logic in the following quote. Not only does it contain more than a grain of uncomfortable truth, it is also a view that is shared by perhaps the majority of our society.

> For a long time this doctrine [original sin] helped to enforce acceptance of the existing social order. For reasons the church could not explain, everyone was born to eternal pain after death unless the church saved them. It carefully monopolised all the sacraments which were the only way to salvation. To be saved, a man had to accept the church's teaching on the way secular society should be organised; if that society ever needed restraining or reforming, the only ways of doing this that the church permitted were admonishment and excommunication. Leaders of church and state often came from the same families; and before a poor man was elevated to any rank in the church, he had to accept its teaching on secular society. Those who wouldn't, whether clerical or lay, were handed over to the state to be tortured or burned. This vividly demonstrated to everyone else the eternal hell in which all dissent would be punished. God is a secular mechanism, a device of class rule. (*Plays One*)

Is it possible for the Church to shake off this oppressive image?

Some say that the only way is to dismantle the old structures and create new ones. Well, maybe, but anyone who's been around the 'new church' scene for a while can attest that they are often as full of traditions and authoritarianism as the most hide-bound cathedral. The traditions are new ones, that's all. Authority may be held by a man in a Hawaiian beach shirt rather than a long frock, but it's just as controlling for all that.

Others would answer that the only way is to have no structures at all. 'I can be a Christian without going to church.' Well maybe, but the first thing Jesus did was to establish a group of followers and the last thing he did was ensure it would continue. And humans are social animals – even if every church were abolished tomorrow, the day afterwards someone would start a club for people who don't go to church any more and the day after that someone would organise a committee and a set of rules!

Yet others, echoing John Lennon, Richard Dawkins and a whole clutch of post-modern philosophers, would say that the whole thing is impossible anyway. They would draw on Nietzsche's idea that any claim to possess absolute truth is an invalid assertion of power. Anyone who claims to have capital-T Truth must by definition be on a power trip. Anyone who believes they know God must, by definition, be mad, bad or an oppressor.

It's a tempting argument. Except that Jesus did and he wasn't.

But the world at large isn't looking at Jesus, it is looking at organised religion. It is looking at us (*not* listening to us) and evaluating Christianity on what it sees. And what it sees is not necessarily what we wish to show it – all of us 'read' far more of what is going on inside others than we consciously recognise.

I believe this issue of religious control and authority is a huge one (and in the wake of September 11, even more so) – so much so that it may seriously decide the fate of organised Christianity in the Western world in this century. I also believe that the answer is there, staring us in the face, in the pages of the Gospels. The way for the Church to shake off its oppressive image is simple – look at the words and actions of its founder and let them sink into our lives. Simple – but radical, and far from easy!

GROUP SESSION

Show video   **5 min.**
Beginning of film, under opening credits: in church, wind blows door; Vianne's arrival.

Discuss   **25–35 min.**
1. The village of Lasquenet like many small communities was locked into tradition. What was *good* about the traditional way the village functioned?
2. *Tranquillité* doesn't seem such a bad thing – after all, who doesn't want life to be safe, secure and calm? But what damage is done by this sort of *tranquillité* – the need to maintain an ordered uncontroversial life at all costs? What unhealthy situations did it lead to in the film?
3. How would you evaluate your church and/or local community on a *tranquillité* scale: too much, not enough, just right?
4. *Chocolat* gives voice to a common view in our society: the Church (indeed all religion) is to be mistrusted because it so often leads to oppression. Clearly this is not what Christ had in mind – equally clearly there is ample evidence for this view. So what is it about communities of faith and their leaders that

makes them tend so easily towards abuse of authority?
(Possible supplementary question if needed.)

5. What might change if Christ turned up at your church or in your community?

Show video   **5 min.**
Outside shop, Guillaume with dog meets widow Audel; Comte visits hairdressers; Comte and priest in graveyard.

Brainstorm   **15–20 min.**
Involve the whole group in answering, write down answers and display them if possible on a board or pinned-up sheet of paper.

6. 'If you lived in this village, you understood what was expected of you, you knew your place in the scheme of things.' In the film, who controls and who allows themselves to be controlled?

7. What do we learn from the film about these characters' backgrounds that might explain why they behave the way they do?

8. In the film, what techniques and tools do the 'controllers' use to *intimidate*? What other ways have you experienced that people have used to intimidate you or others?

9. In the film, how do those who refuse to be intimidated demonstrate their defiance? Are there any other useful ways you have learned to stand up to bullies?

Meditation   **10–15 min.**

Reader 1: Matthew 23:1–12, 23–8

Silence   *(3–5 min.)*
In the silence, ask God to show you any issues of inappropriate control in your life.

Reader 2:

When the north wind blows the church door open, the Comte de Reynaud is quick to shut it. Does he even notice the searing light outside? Does he think of anything but keeping his world safe and contained, keeping things the way he feels they should be?

Pause

When Vianne, the mysterious stranger, comes to the village, she knocks on a door. If she is welcomed, it may change everything.

Pause

When Christ, in John's vision in Revelation, spoke to a church that was comfortable and safe, he said this: 'Those whom I love, I rebuke and discipline. So be earnest, and repent. Here I am! I stand at the door and knock. If anyone hears my voice and opens the door, I will come in and eat with him and he with me' (3:19–20).

Pause

Christ also said: 'I have come that they may have life, and have it to the full' (John 10:10).

Silence   *(1–2 min.)*

Reader 3: Prayer:

Lord,
Help us to open the door – to allow the wind of the
    Spirit to blow through our stuffy lives.
Help us to open the door – to welcome strangers and
    intruders who may just be Christ in disguise.
Help us to open the door – to changes and disturbances
    that may just have something to teach us.
Help us, Lord, to open the door to you. Amen.

Silence *(optional)*   *(1 min.)*

TO CONTINUE YOUR THINKING

During the writing of this booklet, my eye fell on some old newspaper put on the bathroom floor as protection while the room was being decorated. Since our family lives in the real world rather than *Changing Rooms*, it had been there for some time. The paper was dated a few days after the dramatic events of 11 September 2001 and it showed a cartoon of Bush and Blair trying to look Churchillian, but succeeding in looking rather more like monkeys. The speech box above their heads said, 'We shall not flag or fail. We shall go on to the end. We shall fight somebody or other on the beaches, in the fields and on the hills of somewhere or other ... We shall never surrender.'

When our *tranquillité* is threatened, our first thought is to try and reassert control. And in order to do that we need an enemy. We need something or someone to fight – whether or not the blame really lies there and whether or not fighting will solve the problem. And it must be external – the last thing we want to do if we are feeling insecure is to admit that some of the problem might possibly lie within.

The Comte de Reynaud knew this. He was no fool, says the film's narrator, and he knew that even if he achieved the drunken Serge's rehabilitation, that alone would not be enough for him to regain control of the town. 'Some greater problem needed to be identified and solved.' And of course, conveniently, the river rats came sailing up the river and gave him the enemy without.

Read Matthew 23:1–12, 23–8

Since he was a twelve-year-old visiting the Temple, Jesus had observed the religious leaders of his day. He had seen them struggling to hold on to their Judaic authority in a society where the real power lay with a conquering army with quite different gods. And he saw, not just the absurd lengths to which this need for control led them, but what the essential problem was. They thought that if they could sort out the externals, then the internal would be solved too. Jesus knew that it had to be the other way around – they had to clean the inside first.

And Jesus had something even more radical to say – if you really wanted to change things then the solution lay not in trying to hold on to control, but in voluntarily giving it away. It lay in being a servant.

Dangerous ideas and, of course, ones that made Jesus himself immediately become the enemy without.

Pause for thought
Who or what do you see as 'the enemy without' in your life? Is there any way in which the problem may lie within yourself? Is it even a problem to which it is possible to attach blame?

Week Four:
Getting Real – The Power of Acceptance

TO START YOU THINKING

Accepting difference

Time was when Britain was a Christian country. By that I don't mean that everyone was moral and pious and worshipped regularly. Rather that you were either moral, pious and worshipful within a Christian framework, or you were not. Whether you lived within its boundaries or without, Christianity was all that was on offer.

Now it is different. There are substantial numbers of people in our country who believe quite different things from us. We cannot share the same island without respecting them. And we can, and often do, leave our island and discover for ourselves countries which are quite *other* – in their beliefs, their customs, their attitudes. We have made the shocking discovery that it is possible to be moral, pious and worshipful without being Christian.

Not only are we exposed to other religions, but to those who embrace beliefs, practices and spirituality outside the framework of any organised religion at all. The New Age movement has ushered in a myriad of remedies, therapies and cosmologies, and Christians are sharply divided in their reactions to them. There are those who feel that anything that comes with a New Age label must be demonic, others who believe that at worst these alternatives are misguided and at best helpful tools in the Christian quest for the spiritual.

Recently I visited Kuala Lumpur. In the middle of this teeming cosmopolitan Muslim capital was something very odd – a row of mock Tudor villas round a cricket green. It was, of course, where the British lived and ruled back in colonial days and you will find similar 'outposts of empire' all over the parts of the map that were once coloured pink. You may also find more contemporary variants in places like the Costa del Sol with its Red Lion pubs and fish and chip shops. This is one way of living with difference – to retreat into your own tight 'expat' community, to cling to your traditions and to become 'us', carefully insulated from 'them'.

In the UK, practising Christians are now pretty much 'expats' within their own land. We are a minority and very often our reaction has been to huddle together, cling to our traditions and minimise our contact with anyone who might threaten us.

To be a minority is threatening. And to be a minority in matters of belief is even more threatening. Belief is by its nature fragile. It deals with things that cannot be seen or touched or proved. And it is precious and personal, at the centre of our being. We would be strange believers, then, if we never felt threatened by those whose beliefs were different from ours. To feel threatened by difference is a natural reaction. It is what we do with those threatened feelings that matters.

Dealing with difference is never easy. But dealt with it must be, or the Church will gradually retreat into a world of unreality, like wheezing, retired colonels taking tiffin. There are some who say it already has done! This is doubly difficult where issues of faith are concerned, because they have to be dealt with on two levels. On one level there is the objective evaluation of the belief or practice itself. Is it untrue, or simply a different way of saying the same thing? Is it harmful, or just unfamiliar? And on another level there is the need to deal with our threatened feelings. How can I evaluate objectively when it raises so many uncomfortable questions within me? Even if I believe this practice is wrong, how am I going to love and respect the person who practises it?

At root perhaps the question revolves not around *what* we believe in, but *whom*. If we have learned to trust a loving God, who not only made but invades the whole of life, if we have learned to follow in the footsteps of a humble, forgiving Christ – then very little can threaten us. We can embrace those of other faiths without losing our own. We can begin to celebrate and explore difference rather than fear it.

Read John 4:4–26

Jesus was not afraid to talk to someone from a different ethnic and religious group – and a woman of dubious morals, to boot! When he started getting too close for comfort on personal matters, she was quick to divert him on to more general religious controversy (a common technique). Jesus did not ignore the controversy or give way on his belief, but he was quick to turn it round to the essence of the matter – not *where* you worshipped or *what* you did, but *how* you did it.

Pause for thought
Of those from other belief systems whom you have met, whom have you found the most threatening and why?

GROUP SESSION

Show video   **5 min.**
Vianne tells Anouk the story of her grandparents.

Discuss   **10–15 min.**
You may like to divide into groups for both this session

and the following **Ponder and share**. If so, run them both together and allow 5–10 minutes at the end of the combined session to come back together and share conclusions from each group.

1. In the chocolaterie, Vianne does several things that spread an air of mystery – the spinning plate, the hint of secret ingredients, the 'I know your favourite' approach. Do you think these are just a game, a clever marketing ploy, or do they have more sinister undertones? If the latter, what makes you think this?

2. How do you react to Vianne's 'pagan' roots? Do they make you feel curious or uncomfortable? If you met her or someone like her, would you want to know more or would you back off?

3. When you meet someone with a religion or belief system other than your own, do you first look for similarities or differences, and why?

Ponder and share   **10–15 min.**

Take a little time in silence to think about any experiences you have had with other religions or alternative therapies, or even with different brands of Christianity. Share your reactions to that experience:

4. What are the things that have made you feel uncomfortable about them?

5. What have you learned from them?

Brainstorm   **10 min.**

6. On your board or sheet of paper draw two columns: attractive/off-putting. Put yourself in the place of someone in today's society, without a faith of his or her own, 'shopping around' to find something to believe in and somewhere to belong. Imagine yourself in this person's shoes (maybe you can fix on someone you know), as he or she visits different

churches, other faiths and alternative therapies and New Age activities.

Then under each column write down the things you might encounter in the people you met, in the way they practised their faith, the way they behaved towards you, and in the dynamics of the group, that might entice you to get involved or might put you off. (*Optional extra question*)

7. Go through with a highlighter pen and mark those that apply to your church in particular.

Show video 5 min.

Vianne and Armande in the chocolaterie; Vianne meeting Roux 'I'd like to apologise'; Serge apologising to Josephine; public meeting.

Ponder and share 8–15 min.

8. Have you ever 'helped someone to understand they were not welcome'? It may not be as reprehensible as it sounds – the chances are that you have *had to* for one reason or another. If so why? Is there a way of doing so which still respects the person's dignity?

Discuss 5 min.

(*Optional extra question*)

9. Josephine accepted Serge's apology, but she refused to return with him. Was she right to do so?

Brainstorm 8–15 min.

Roux (the river rat), with long experience on the margins of society, expects that people are either going to accuse him, or try and save him: 'Which idea are you selling?' If we have any sort of real belief in the Christian message, then it follows (doesn't it?) that we believe it *can* save people and therefore we do want to share it.

10. What conditions can we put in place to ensure that
    we share our faith in a positive and not a negative way?
    Make a list of attitudes that ensure that, if we do
    share our faith, we do so appropriately and effectively.

Meditation   4–10 min.

Reader 1: Mark 12:28–31 (*optional*)
Ponder in silence (*optional*)   (*3 min.*)
Why do you think that Jesus put loving God as the first
commandment? After all, most of his teaching was
supremely down to earth. Might he not have said that the
most effective way to show your love for God *was* to love
your neighbour? Is there anything about the *process* –
about being in a right relationship with God *first* – that
enables you *then* to relate to your neighbour with a more
loving attitude?

Reader 2:
John Drane, a Christian with much experience of the New
Age movement, writes: 'In the case of every New Ager I
have ever met, I have felt that God could give that person
to the Church as a gift, if only he or she could meet
Christians in whose lives the reality of Christ was an
everyday experience.'

(*Short pause*)

Reader 3:
St Francis of Assisi is said to have told his followers: 'Go
preach the gospel. Use words if necessary.'

Silence   (*30 sec.–1 min.*)

Reader 4:
The following reading shows how radical and revol-

utionary the gospel is. When truly practised, it will be quite evident even without words: Matthew 5:43–8.

Silence *(30 sec.–1 min.)*

Reader 5: Prayer

Lord,
We acknowledge that who we are speaks far louder
than what we say, or even what we do.
Help us to accept ourselves fully
  as God accepts us,
So that we may accept others fully
  as God accepts them.
Help us to forgive ourselves fully
  as God forgives us,
So that we may forgive others fully
  as a token of the forgiveness God wants them to
  receive.
And help us to be quicker to celebrate difference
  than to condemn it.
In the name of the loving, forgiving, accepting Christ,
  Amen.

Silence *(optional)* *(1 min.)*

TO CONTINUE YOUR THINKING

Read Matthew 5:43–8

What on earth does Jesus mean by that last statement in this passage? *'Be perfect.'* To be honest, I'm not sure. (I don't think I've ever come across anyone else who really knew either.)

But I think I can be pretty certain, based on the other

things Jesus said and did, about two things it doesn't mean:

It doesn't mean that only people with an unblemished record can get into the Kingdom of God. Jesus made it clear that he had come not for the righteous but for sinners. He made it clear that God the Father welcomed back prodigals. He told the criminal on the neighbouring cross, 'I tell you the truth, this day you will be with me in paradise' (Luke 23:43).

It doesn't mean that anyone is likely to achieve perfection. Jesus' model prayer makes that clear: 'Forgive us our sins, as we forgive everyone who sins against us. And lead us not into temptation' (Luke 11:3–4). He told the religious leaders of the day that for all their law-keeping they were like 'whitewashed tombs' (Matthew 23:27). He said that prayer was not about telling God how good we were, but about asking mercy for our sins (Luke 18:9–13).

So why did he say it? Was he having a brainstorm? Did the Gospel records get it wrong? Well, as I said, I'm not sure. But one thing I have discovered: these outrageous, unexpected sayings of Jesus have an immense value, because what they do is stop us in our tracks and make us think.

If it's impossible to be perfect, then why advocate it? Well, maybe to make it unequivocally clear that living life God's way is not about achieving a pass mark. There is no 65 per cent pass, 85 per cent distinction. It just doesn't work like that.

Thank goodness it doesn't. For if it did, we would be forever evaluating how well we were doing, trying to gain 'brownie points', checking our grade average – eternally looking inwards.

Read Mark 12:28–31

And the essence of a perfect life, as Jesus makes supremely clear, is about looking upwards and looking outwards.

Yes, there is some looking inwards to be done. Because as Jesus also makes clear, we are to love our neighbours '*as ourselves*'. And in those two words, Jesus demonstrated that he understood, centuries before Freud and Jung had drawn breath, what whole libraries of psychology and self-help books have tried to say since, that in order to love and accept others, you need to love and accept yourself. And to do this you need to know yourself forgiven.

And this is where the circle returns to the beginning. Because in order to love and understand ourselves, in order to love and understand others, we need to know unequivocally that none of us is perfect.

None of us lives our lives with perfect wisdom and compassion. None of us never gets tired or ill or fed up with our nearest and dearest. None of us fulfils our potential. None of us has a perfect grasp of the truth.

Years ago, my father said something that stuck in my mind. He remarked that if we did meet someone perfect, we'd never recognise it.

I think he was probably right. Because when it comes to it, we have a pretty odd idea of what perfect is. We expect the physique of Michelangelo's David, the brains of Einstein, the charm of Princess Diana, the compassion of Mother Teresa, etc. We make an assumption that perfect people would be good at everything, that their bodies and their behaviour would conform to some norm of beauty. Perfection would mean perfect conformity. And so, not surprisingly, we all secretly feel that if we did meet someone perfect, we would instantly dislike her or him.

I think, though, that what my dad was trying to say was that perfection would mean being perfectly and wholly yourself, quite unique in how you looked and what you did and thought and said. (I have since discovered that the original Greek word for 'perfection' used in this verse has more to do with maturity and fulfilment than with being unblemished, so it would seem to bear this out.)

I don't think any of us totally achieves this maturity. I

suspect, though, that the ones who come nearest to it are those who would never in a million years imagine themselves to be so. Those who are so accepting of themselves – of their gifts and strengths and of their flaws and failures – that they can happily get on with looking upwards and outwards without thinking about it. I suspect that the ones who come nearest to perfection are not the ones we envy most, but the ones who most make us feel good about ourselves.

And I bet, although I have no theological evidence to support this, that if we did meet someone perfect, one evidence would be their ability to laugh at themselves.

Pause for thought
Look around you, as you go about your daily life this week, for those who may be nearer to perfection than you had ever suspected.

Week Five:
Growing Up – The Process of Change

TO START YOU THINKING

I want you for a few minutes to take an imaginary journey with me, and with some of the characters of *Chocolat*.

Picture Paul de Reynaud as a chubby seven-year-old in short trousers, stiff collar and tie, with hair slicked down ready for mass. 'One day you will be Comte de Reynaud,' his mother tells him, 'and upon you the moral welfare of this village will rest.' Picture him, passing each day the statue of his ancestor in the square and seeing that steely gaze of responsibility, falling, it seems, on him alone.

Picture Josephine, a teenager giggling as the boys pass by, full of dreams for the future. Watch as it gradually dawns on her that her father is a collaborator with the hated Nazis. See her shame as the Germans withdraw and her father is dragged into the square to be spat upon and beaten. Picture her, forever tainted, her dreams dashed, reaching out for some glittering jewel left behind in a bombed house. Just for a moment it stills the ache in her heart.

Picture Caroline, a gawky eleven-year-old in the high school gym. 'Sorry,' says her new friend, 'my mum says I can't come to tea with you.' Caroline knows why. She knows what they say about her mother. Armande Voisin – the slut. She swears, reads dirty books, drinks with the men, never does any housework. Worst of all – she says exactly what she thinks. 'When I am older,' vows Caroline, 'I'll never put my children through this.'

Picture nine-year-old Vianne on yet another rattling bus, journeying to yet another unknown town. 'It's fun,' her mother tells her. 'We're not like those other people. We are wanderers. This is our life.' See Vianne as she presses her nose to the glass and conjures that ever dimmer memory of the man who seemed so kind and gentle. Her father – one of those other people. 'Yes, maman,' says Vianne. 'It's going to be fun.'

When we are small children, our parents are God to us. As we grow, we discover they are sometimes wrong. By the time we are teenagers, we are quite likely to think they are wrong about everything! But still they leave with us an immense heritage of ideas, attitudes and emotions – things so deeply ingrained that we never question them. Indeed, we probably don't even know they are there – until one day something or someone comes along to challenge them.

There are two ways of dealing with this subconscious legacy. One is to try and dig it all up. Bring the whole lot to the surface, examine every bit of it. The other is to keep it all deeply buried. To stamp it down. To cover it over, the moment it threatens to pierce the surface.

The first way is costly – in time and probably in money (this is not a task to be undertaken alone) – and although it may reap dividends in terms of increased self-knowledge and there may be times when it becomes a desperate necessity, it also runs the risk of exposing things you are not yet equipped to deal with.

The second is also likely to be costly – certainly in terms of mental wellbeing and quite possibly in terms of physical health. Its benefit is that on the surface things keep running smoothly. There are times when life is just too demanding for introspection. But it can be rather like tiptoeing around a minefield. If you don't know what is buried, then you never know when anything is likely to explode.

Thankfully, as I have gone on in the Christian life, I have discovered that these are not the *only* two ways. For if you have given your life into God's hands, then you can trust God to bring these hidden attitudes and emotions to the surface at the right time, at a time when you are ready to deal with them. It becomes possible to welcome those challenging intruders as friends, rather than resenting them as enemies. Because you are no longer facing them alone.

Of course, it will never *feel* like the right time. It will never *feel* comfortable and cosy when the deepest things about us are challenged. But if you are committed to growth, if you are learning to trust God as a loving Parent who wants only good things for his children, then it at least becomes possible to ride those feelings, to hang on in there and trust that God is a specialist in bringing strength out of weakness and joy out of pain.

Read John 3:1-8; Matthew 18:1-3

These readings can provoke many thoughts and be interpreted in many ways, but one thing Jesus seems to be saying is that it is possible to begin again. No, we cannot enter again into our mother's womb. We may not be able to undo our parenting and our background culture, but we can release its hold on us. We can become new people. We can see the world through childlike eyes again. It is not only possible, Jesus implies, but necessary. To be fully the people God wants us to be, we have to take off our adult straitjacket and become willing to learn.

Pause for thought

Ask God whether there is anything from your past that is quite near the surface right now and ready to be dealt with. Perhaps you will need to look at your present tensions, reactions and emotions and ask yourself if they have their roots in something from your past. If something does come to mind, look at it for a while, but then commit it into God's hands. Ask God to deal with any shame or blame, but to show you also what strengths and blessings your past has given you.

GROUP SESSION

Show video   **5 min.**
Caroline mends bike; Armande's funeral; Vianne drawn
by mother's ashes; Caroline and Comte, 'No one would
think less of you . . .'

Brainstorm   **10 min.**
Many of the characters in *Chocolat* grow up in the course
of the film. But in order to do so, they have to acknowledge their need to change. The following will probably
work best by taking a character and going through all
four questions, before moving on to the next character.

1. Which characters grew up in the film, and what did
   they have to acknowledge in order for the process
   of change to start?
2. What was the point at which this process of change
   began for each of them?
3. And then what action did they each take to demonstrate change?
4. For many of these characters it meant stepping out
   from under some inappropriate control on their lives.
   Who did this and who were the controlling characters whose influence they needed to shake off?

Reader 1: John 8:1–11   **2 min.**

Discuss   **10–15 min.**
Jesus pointed out only the difference between this woman
and her accusers. She had broken the 'eleventh commandment' – *'Thou shalt not get caught'*. Her shame was public
while theirs remained private.

5. How do you react when you hear that someone
   'respectable' has a shameful secret?
   Think about a few famous people whose secrets
   have come to light: Jeffrey Archer, Princess Diana,

Jonathan Aitken, Michael Barrymore. How do you react to them? Is there a difference and if so why?

6. How have you reacted when someone you knew admitted his or her failure or weakness to you? Has it strengthened or weakened your relationship? Has it strengthened or weakened your respect for him or her?

Reader 2: John 13:37–8; 18:25–7   **3 min.**
Reader 3: John 21:15–19

Ponder and share   **10–15 min.**
Jesus made it clear that failure did not mean you had no future. Perhaps he knew that failure and shame could be as much a means of grace and growth as the most wonderful blessing.

7. Take some time to think about any occasions in your life when you feel you failed, or when you had to admit your weakness in front of others. In which ways has that experience made you a stronger or better person?

8. You may like to look at the question the other way round: think about a time when you grew most, in responsibility, in courage, in spiritual stature, etc. What precipitated that change? Did the growth come from strength or from weakness?

After a few moments' silence, and if you feel you can, share your thoughts in small groups.

Show video   **5 min.**
Père Henri's sermon; festival; Vianne throws ashes away.
   In this clip, look out for images that could have some Christian symbolism.

Discuss   **10–15 min.**
9. Did you notice any images with close links to

Christian symbolism? If so, what were they? What might these have to say to us about our own process of growth?

Christian doctrine states that Christ was the Son of God and the Son of Man, fully human and fully divine. However, since that is an almost impossible concept to comprehend, most Christians tend to major on one or the other.

10. Do you think that you as an individual, or you as a church, tend to focus more on Christ's divinity or on his humanity?

11. What difference would it make if the balance shifted? Are there any dangers in going too far one way or the other?

Meditation   4–8 min.

Silence   *(3–5 min.)*

In the silence, think back over the whole of this Lent Course. Note the things that stick in your mind. Perhaps note also the things you would rather not think about!

Pause

Ask God to show you if there are any lessons you need to learn or put into practice, or any ways in which you need to grow.

Reader 4: Prayer

Lord our Lord,
Whose full divinity was seen in your full humanity,
Send the wind of your Spirit to stir us to change,
Send the fire of your Spirit to lighten our spirits,
Send the dove of your Spirit to help us be at peace with ourselves.
Take our weaknesses and turn them into opportunities.
Take our shame and use it to make us strong.

Help us to be fully human

That in being fully who you made us to be, the divine
 might enter in.

In the name of the mysterious, troublesome, healing and
 affirming Christ,

Amen.

Silence *(1–2 min.)*

Share **3–6 min.**

In small groups (pairs or triplets are probably best), share
briefly something that you have learned from the course
and intend to take away with you. Still in small groups,
take a few moments to pray for each other, either out
loud or in silence.

TO CONTINUE YOUR THINKING

Lighten up

When I came to write these concluding words, I asked
myself, 'What message has doing this course left with me?
What message would I most like people to take away with
them?' The answer that came into my head and lodged
there, somewhat unexpectedly, was this: 'Lighten up'.

That's a bit rich, isn't it? I hear you say. *Haven't we just
been talking about change and growth, and confronting subconscious attitudes and inappropriate control, and loving
your neighbour and self-denial? Not exactly lightweight. And
aren't we just coming up to Easter and Jesus on the cross
and pain and blood and death and sin and all that stuff?*

All true.

But it seems to me that the picture *Chocolat* paints of
church is as a place full of grey, guilty, burdened people,
straitjacketed by convention. In contrast, Vianne's

chocolaterie was a place of lightness and ease. It was a place people were listened to rather than talked at. It was a place of acceptance and fun. And because of that, it was a place where people blossomed.

And even though that is all a bit caricatured and simplistic, my experience of life in several churches tells me there is more than a grain of truth there. Church is not often the first place people think of when they are looking for love and acceptance.

But that is not how it should be.

If you visited some of those churches of my experience, you might wonder what I meant. After all, I have spent a great deal of my Christian life in the sort of churches where people wear casual clothes and sing to guitars and drums and clap their hands and even sometimes dance. I have been in churches where people are genuinely warm and caring and committed to each other, where they are genuinely trying to shake off tradition. They certainly don't appear straitjacketed places.

But it seems to me that wherever faith becomes an organisational thing, be it in the most traditional cathedral or the most right-on charismatic fellowship, then it is likely to be subject to controlling influences, a pressure to conform, and a sort of constant drip, drip, drip of guilt-inducing 'Could do better' from the pulpit. Often this is unintentional. If not, then it is mostly the result of well-intentioned zeal. And yes, just now and then, I have been aware of more malign forces at work.

Do I mean then that we should abandon organised religion?

No. I believe that Jesus intended his followers to be banded together, that God wants Christians to be community and that we can serve the world better together than apart.

But I do think that very many Christians need to lighten up.

I think church should be a place where people blossom.

And I think it can be. I have seen it happen – many, many times. Discovering that God loves you and accepts you is the most wonderful liberating experience it is possible to have.

But sometimes I have seen these same people go on to wilt under the pressure of what others are telling them they now ought to be and do and think.

Christianity should be about relieving guilt, not inducing it. It should be about relieving burdens, not piling them on. I am not saying this because I want to change the nature of Christianity, but because that is what Christ always intended. And because that is what is there, built into the very fabric of Christianity itself. Repentance and confession are intended to lift the guilt, not pile it on. Holy Communion is intended to be a gift not a duty.

A couple of years ago I went to a Communion service in Salisbury Cathedral. It just happened that I had seen the film *Billy Elliot* the night before. The atmosphere of the cathedral inspired me – the deep harmonies of the organ echoing around ancient stone, the exquisite choirboy voices soaring up to the magnificent arched ceiling, the glow of light through stained glass. But when it came to Communion, I looked at us – solid, respectable, middle-aged, approaching the altar stiffly and reverently with lowered eyes – and it all seemed so wrong.

We should have been tap-dancing down that long aisle, running and leaping and twirling and kicking like Billy Elliot. There should have been a jazz band and trumpets and a chorus of angels jiving above us. Because what we were actually celebrating was so amazing. God loves us. Enough to die for us. He wants us to be free and strong and forgiven.

No, I didn't start tap-dancing. (But maybe it's not too late to learn.)

Read Matthew 11:28–30

These three verses have been haunting me for months.

What does it mean to take on Christ's yoke? What can I learn from him about living under a *light* yoke? Following are just a few thoughts on the subject:

- We are designed for activity and work.
- But Christ does not intend us to live weary, burdened lives.
- Therefore we need to learn a new lighter and easier way of being.
- We need to resist being dumped on by others.
- The trick is only to take on what we believe Christ wants of us.
- The secret is in being gentle and humble of heart.
- Living humbly for Christ relieves us of the burden of always having to get it right.

I don't think I've yet discovered all these verses have to tell me – but I'm still looking. Perhaps you too would benefit from reading and rereading this simple appeal from Jesus, letting it sink into you until you begin to grasp what it means to live under his light yoke.

Give joy room to flourish

When I tested the part of the course that talks about having fun, someone said to me, 'But you haven't mentioned joy.' No, I didn't, because you can't manufacture joy. You can create fun, you can create welcome, you can create pleasure – but you can't create joy. Joy is a by-product. Telling Christians they *ought* to be joyful is about as silly as telling newborn babies they *ought* to be able to talk.

But you can, I believe, create an environment which allows joy to flourish. I think both the film *Chocolat* and the words of the Gospels have some clues on how to do that. I hope that as you go on to celebrate Easter, you will have begun to catch a glimpse of what that might mean.

Postscript

The priest and writer Gerard W. Hughes describes 'the longest and most difficult journey in the world' as 'the journey from the top layer of our minds to the heart . . .' (*Oh God, Why?*).

What he means is that it is relatively easy to take an idea into your thinking, but not at all easy to incorporate it into the depths of your being – to your gut reactions, to how you live.

It may be that there are things in this Lent course that have provoked you to think. You may have considered ideas that you would like to take further. But it may also be that – like an awful lot of things that go on in church: Lent courses, Bible studies, sermons – it will have drifted out of your consciousness even before you step out of the door.

It is hardly surprising.

If you had been a Christian a hundred and fifty years ago, then it is quite likely that the only intellectual stimulation you got from week to week would have been at church. No television, no Internet, no phone, no emails, no radio, no films, no junk mail, maybe a personal letter or two, maybe the odd book or newspaper, but nothing like the amount of words and images that bombard us daily in the twenty-first century. You probably worked at some manual labour – scrubbing the laundry, ploughing the fields, at the coal face, in the factory – work that gave you plenty of time to contemplate and digest any ideas that did come your way. Whether that was a better or worse lifestyle than today is beside the point. It was different, hugely different.

It is true that a large amount of the words and images that are thrown at us today are junk: junk mail, junk TV, junk films, junk novels, junk worship songs, junk preaching. (Oh dear, did I say that? If your experience is different, then count yourself lucky.)

But an awful lot is not.

As a writer, I know that whilst ours can be a rewarding profession, it is also extremely tough. You would not put yourself through this rollercoaster existence unless you had something to say about what it means to be human. Admittedly it may have been pummelled or squeezed or stretched by the forces of Mammon in the process, but the chances are that much of what you see on the screen or read in print came originally from the depths of someone's experience and therefore has the potential to speak deeply to you.

And even if sometimes the songs you sing or the preaching you hear lack a certain intellectual rigour or spiritual profundity, then usually they are based on Bible verses that do possess those qualities. You can always go back to source.

I hope that if this Lent course has done nothing else, it may have convinced you that God can speak to you through film. God can speak through anything or anyone, of course, but film is a very potent medium, and ironically the forces of Mammon collude to make it so. The financial resource and human effort needed to make a film is so great, that you simply don't embark on it unless you think that many people will want to engage with it. Since there is only so much you can do with sex and violence and special effects, Hollywood is hungry for stories that engage the human spirit. And good stories, by their nature, are about conflict and journey and change and what it means to be human. Their conclusions may not be Christian ones, but in provoking us to thought and debate, they can provoke God's thoughts in us.

But to return to where I began, how can we ensure that these thoughts take the long journey from the top of our head to the depths of our being?

One thing I'm sure Gerard W. Hughes would endorse is that it takes time. Time apart from all the bombardment of words and images. Time of quiet. Time perhaps when the rhythm of physical exercise or labour stills our mind and allows us to listen.

I can be so certain because it is something he practises. He speaks in his books of having exiled himself for several weeks on an uninhabited Scottish island, of having taken a pilgrimage, walking from England to Rome, both for just that purpose. These remedies may be a bit excessive for you, but you could allow yourself a day here and there, a morning of stillness, an hour for a solitary walk, a few minutes at the beginning of each day.

Another idea he endorses is that of writing things down. Keep a journal of what you read and see and hear. Note the things that seem like God speaking to you. Note also the things that perplex you or confuse you or irritate you. Revisit your journal occasionally and see whether any of those things have begun the downward journey to your heart.

I too endorse these things. I practise them imperfectly, but I can say with honesty that they work.

But then, admittedly, I am both a writer and an introvert. I like writing things down. I like being alone. If these things are not for you (and don't be too quick to decide that they are not), then another discipline that may speed the journey from mind to heart may be simply to speak out. Share the ideas that are stirring in you with someone you trust. Ask him or her to back you up in prayer and to come back to you and enquire on your progress.

How you do it doesn't matter, but above all embark on the journey. (To aid you at this point, I have added some

questions below). It may seem that here I am, just advoca-
ting more things to fit into your already complica-
ted life. But curiously, I am convinced that taking time to
contemplate and sift your thoughts will lighten things up
rather than add to your burdens. Because if you know
clearly in your own heart what things God wants you to
do, then it becomes a whole lot easier to turn aside all
those other demands when they come crashing in.

It is better to hear one word from God and to incorporate it into your being, than to hear hundreds and
thousands of wise words that only ever get as far as the
top of your head.

Jesus had some succinct and witty comments on the
subject, and I can do no better than end with these:

'Therefore everyone who hears these words of mine
and puts them into practice is like a wise man who
built his house on a rock. The rain came down, the
streams rose, and the winds blew and beat about that
house; yet it did not fall, because it had its foundations
on the rock.

'But everyone who hears these words of mine and
does not put them into practice is like a foolish man
who built his house on sand. The rain came down,
the streams rose, and the winds blew and beat against
that house, and it fell with a great crash.' (Matthew
7:24–7)

Pause for thought
*What things, if any, have arisen from this course that I need
to think about further?*
*What things, if any, have arisen from this course that I
don't want to think about?*
*What things, if any, have arisen from this course that irritate
or confuse me?*
*What things, if any, have arisen from this course that I need
to try and put into practice?*

Leader's Notes

BEFORE YOU BEGIN

Showing the film beforehand

The course runs for five sessions, but I strongly recommend that all course participants need to have seen the whole film beforehand. Even if they have seen it some time previously, a viewing just before the course to refresh their memory is pretty important. I suggest therefore organising an introductory session before the course starts in order to view the film.

However, if you are running the course as a whole church activity, there is a problem with this. Although using excerpts from a film during a public meeting is exempt from copyright restrictions and charges, technically showing the whole film in a public viewing is not, even if no charge is made. Make sure your film showing is by invitation only for members of the course, and not a public viewing as such.

Using film excerpts

The timings I have given for the excerpts used are based on the assumption that the video player is set to zero at the opening of the film – i.e. when the words 'Miramax films present' comes up against a black background. **NB**: This is *after* the Miramax logo.

If you do not have a minutes and seconds counter on

your recorder, you will need to work out the 'In' and 'Out' points for yourself, based on your own machine's counter. Even if you do have a real time counter, it might be well to double-check the timings on your own machine – in my experience there seem to be slight variations, especially when fast forwarding.

Make sure that the video is set up ready for the first clip *before* the session begins. The second clip is trickier, but try to get as near as you can just by using the counter, without fast forwarding on screen. Try and have a quick practice of this beforehand, to avoid disrupting the meeting too much by spooling back and forth. If you are really a technical klutz like me and find this too difficult, then you could settle on using only one of the clips during the session, and describe the action and quote the script for the other.

Knowing the film

As I said in the general introduction, you as leader might do well to see the film through at least twice beforehand, in order to really absorb its detail and nuances. You will probably need to familiarise yourself with the character names (see p. 4) and it may even be helpful to the whole group to have them written up on a board for general reference. However, to help you further, I have given some prompt answers in the leader's notes for that session to cover any points you may have missed.

Knowing your group

I have tried to make the group outlines as user-friendly as possible, but please feel free to adapt as needed for your particular group. You will probably find that in groups larger than six or eight discussion might be difficult, or at least some people will find it harder to take part. You will notice that there is a minimum and maximum time for each activity. Keeping to the minimum time will give you an approximate one-hour session, while using the maximum times will result in the session lasting an hour and a half.

Setting your boundaries

It may be wise, certainly at the beginning of the whole course and perhaps at the beginning of every session, to refer to the boundaries needed to create a 'safe environment' (Introduction, pp. 4–5): *confidentiality, respect* and *genuine listening*. It may also be worth repeating the definition of *community*. As there is so much material in these sessions, it may be important to stress that each person keep their contributions fairly brief.

Within these sessions there is the potential to deviate into other subjects: New Age, sharing your faith, others' view of the church, etc. This course is much more about individuals' personal reactions and growth, than about beliefs and structures. However, it may well provoke issues that ideally could be followed up at a later date. Make a note of these, and if appropriate, refer the group to the References and Resources section at the back of the book, which suggests some ideas for further reading.

Addressing deep issues

It became apparent during some of the trial sessions of the course that some questions were touching on deep issues in people's lives. One member very wisely suggested that it was important not to raise painful or difficult matters and then leave them hanging in mid air. Out of this came the suggestion that individual prayer could be offered at the end of each meeting, should anyone need it. From that point on we adopted this practice, and I suggest you do the same.

Although it will probably be too late at the end of an evening meeting to spend more than a very short time in prayer, it may be an opening for further listening, befriending and prayer to take place at a later time. If it becomes apparent that the person needs rather deeper counselling, then be sure to arrange for him or her to see someone qualified and experienced in that area.

Throwing a party

At the end of the trial run of this course, our group decided it would be fun to hold a *Chocolat* party. It took the form of a chocolate feast – a three-course meal with all three courses containing chocolate! You might think that that was unbearably rich and unpalatable, but in fact, with high-cocoa-content chocolate used sparingly, it was delicious, and such a good time was had that it began to convince me there might be something in the argument for chocolate as a 'mind-altering substance' after all!

In our case, it was just a fun ending to the course, but if, during the series, some of the discussions about hospitality and welcoming strangers have taken root, you might like to follow them up by using it as a way of inviting others in.

Or just as an Easter celebration – I don't know how Christ would feel about us using chocolate to celebrate his resurrection, but I have a hunch he might be delighted to join the party. (See pp. 86ff., 'Ideas for a Chocolate Feast'.)

Week One:
Giving Up – A Prelude to Change

Show video
In: Just *after* Caroline ' . . . mistake. I just told you that you made one'; farmhouse at night.   15 min. 20 sec.
Out:
On back view of three widows walking down road.

                                              18 min. 42 sec.

2. One thing that is worth pointing out is how drab these people's lives are. They have given up trying to brighten their lives.

3. Think about the form of the service and where the emphases lie. Think also about visual impressions, both of the place and the people. Think about what is *not* there as well as what is.

Brainstorm

You will need a large pad of paper, a felt tip pen and a highlighter pen for this. Try and get people to contribute answers as quickly as possible.

Show video

In: Comte and Serge crossing the village square.

45 min. 39 sec.

Out: ' . . . some greater problem needed to be identified and solved.' 49 min. 50 sec.

8. Clue A – two dogs attempting to mate; Clue B – the film (unlike the book) is set in 1959, just as the Swinging Sixties and the pill are about to make an appearance.

9. People may have strong opinions on this and it might be necessary to stress that there are no 'right answers'. Or perhaps that the right answer is not *either/or* but *both*.

10. Matthew 4:1–11, 18–22.

11. Mark 10:17–27.

For both these questions, you need to have read the passages beforehand and be familiar enough with them to explain the incidents in question, in case group members have not had enough time to do the homework for themselves. Stress that this is an exercise in imagination.

Week Two:
Giving Out – The Power of a Gift

Show video

It might be better to ask question 1 before showing the clip.

In: Just after Anouk at school: 'You don't have a father.' 'Sure I do, we just don't know who he is.' First words: Armande: 'I was out all night with him . . .'   24 min. 52 sec.

Play to the point where Vianne leaves the bar and Josephine smells the chocolate in her hands (29 min. 24 sec.). Then if preferred fast forward through the scenes where Luke sketches the bird and Vianne goes to see the Comte. Come back in for Vianne greeting Josephine outside shop. 'How long have you been standing here?' (32 min. 30 sec.)

Out: Josephine: 'You make the most wonderful chocolate.'
    35 min. 05 sec.

1. Ways in which Vianne offers love and acceptance:
   - She gives Armande the gift of listening.
   - She is interested enough to ask about Armande's needs: 'You have a problem?'
   - She gives Josephine a gift of chocolates (despite knowing she has stolen?).
   - She actively seeks out Josephine and refuses to be put off by Serge.
   - She indicates that she understands Josephine's kleptomania but still accepts her: 'I know'.
   - She asks Josephine's advice, 'Do me a favour, try one of these rose creams . . .'
   - She stops and looks at Luc's drawing and praises it.
   - She doesn't try to tell Josephine where she is wrong: 'No, I don't think you're stupid.'
   - She respects Josephine enough to accept her point of view, even though she realises it is wrong: 'Then it must be true, my mistake.'

2. Off-putting ways in which Armande and Josephine behaved:
   - When Vianne first turns up at Armande's she is greeted rudely, 'Who the hell are you?' (4 min. 50 sec.)
   - Despite the terrible condition of the old patisserie, Armande stomps off telling Vianne to keep it in good condition.
   - When Armande first comes to the chocolaterie (22 min. 32 sec.) she is rude and abrupt.
   - When Josephine first comes in (17 min. 36 sec.) she steals, is unfriendly and mutters to herself. She has previously been glimpsed outside the window and been described as 'waltzing to her own tune'.
   - When Vianne visits Josephine, she is not welcoming: 'What do you want?' . . . 'I don't have friends. Does Serge know you're here?' (Also Serge's reaction to Vianne's visit might put her off getting involved with Josephine.) Josephine shows fear at the visit, both fear of Serge and fear of the Comte. It might be worth pointing out that we learn later that the Comte owns the bar and they are just tenants.

3. Reactions to difficult people might include:
   - fear;
   - anger, irritation, annoyance;
   - they seem to highlight your own failings;
   - embarrassment: not knowing what to say or how to deal with them;
   - concern that if you are seen to be friends with socially unacceptable people, you might become socially unacceptable yourself.

Show video
In: Armande dressed up in her party hat (just after food preparation, wind starts to blow, chocolate being stirred).
                                          1 hr 12 min. 57 sec.

Out: Caroline arrives on river bank to see them dancing on boat.   1 hr 17 min. 15 sec.

Meditation

'Teach me to dance' comes from the album *From a Spark to a Flame* by Graham Kendrick. Also found in *Songs of Fellowship* volume 2. You may prefer to play the song, or sing it together as an end to the meeting.

NB: Don't forget to suggest that if the session has brought anything up that people would like to talk over or pray over, they can approach leaders or someone else they trust at the end.

Week Three:
Getting Wise – The Possibility of Change

Show video

In: Just before narration begins: 'Once upon a time . . .'
                                                            1 min. 06 sec.
Out: Just after Vianne knocks on the door.
                                                            4 min. 34 sec.

4. I used the phrase 'communities of faith' because I wanted to widen it to all religious groups, not just churches, but perhaps it is the 'faith' aspect rather than the 'communities' that is more important. Try and tease out what it is about *spiritual* authority that makes a difference, e.g. a priest by wearing robes and offering the bread and wine takes on a role as mediator between God and humanity. It is very easy therefore to see the priest in a 'god' role generally. A preacher may tell his or her flock that 'God says . . .' and therefore takes on the role of mouthpiece of God. This may be valid in, for instance, a straight quote

from Scripture, but it may also be a way of manipulating the congregation into certain actions or viewpoints. And because Christians so much *want* their church to reflect the Kingdom of God, they can be very reluctant to question, expose malpractice or rock the boat in any way.

Show video
In: Widows looking in shop window.   18 min. 13 sec.
Out: Just after: 'important to know one's enemy'.
                                                22 min. 17 sec.

NB: In each of the following four questions, I have tried to include every possible answer I could think of. However, don't feel you have to extract every one of them from the group, or run through them all yourself. Use as appropriate.

6. **Who allows themselves to   Who controls**:
   be controlled:

Parishioners	Comte de Reynaud
Père Henri	Comte de Reynaud
Josephine	Serge
Anouk	Vianne
Luc	Caroline – his mother

7. **Clues from the characters' backgrounds:**
   Comte
   • His shame at his wife leaving him leads him to divert attention by looking for shame and blame in other situations (and perhaps the free and easy Vianne reminds him of his wife).
   • He bears the weight of his heritage. He has probably been told that he should live up to his illustrious ancestors and been brought up to think of himself as guardian of the town's morals.

Caroline

- Her mother Armande tells Vianne that Caroline never used to be so protective of the boy before her husband died (25 min. 58 sec.). She is terrified of losing her son and mother as she has previously lost her husband (presumably to illness).

Josephine

- Serge tells the Comte that Josephine's father was a collaborator with the Germans and that no one else would have her (44 min. 00 sec.). Josephine has been brought up to live with shame.

Serge

- The scene in the catechism class (45 min. 59 sec.) shows us that Serge is none too bright and possibly illiterate. Perhaps that is why he has turned to violence as a way of proving himself.

8. Techniques which the controllers use to intimidate:

Comte

- We are shown that he is the landlord for both the hairdressers (20 min. 11 sec.) and the bar (and presumably also for other places in the village) so he has economic power over the villagers.
- He plays on Père Henri's youth and inexperience, insists on correcting his sermons, and uses the example of the previous long-serving priest to intimidate him (21 min. 33 sec.).
- He uses Père Henri's sermons to play on the parishioners' sense of guilt and religious fear: 'Satan has many guises . . . for what could seem more harmless than chocolate?' (1 hr 07 min. 23 sec.)
- He is not above a well-placed slanderous bit of gossip. In the hairdressers: 'My heart goes out to that poor illegitimate child of hers' (20 min. 53 sec.).
- He plays on people's social fears in trying to get rid of the 'river rats': 'These people . . . would contami-

nate the spirit of our quiet town, the innocence of
our children . . .' (55 min. 58 sec.).

Serge
- Physical violence.

Vianne and Caroline
- Parents of course have a right and a duty to control
  their children. The problem lies in doing it in the
  child's best interest and in knowing how to permit
  more freedom gradually as the child gets older.

9. Demonstrations of defiance:

Père Henri
- Eventually seizes the opportunity to deliver the
  sermon he wants to preach.

Josephine
- Leaves Serge.
- Hits him over the head with the skillet.
- Refuses to go back.

Luc
- Meets Armande, his grandmother, at the choc-
  olaterie.
- Goes to Armande's party.

Anouk
- Fights against moving on again.

Vianne
- Makes it clear she does not conform to the Comte's
  values: tells him right away that she is unmarried
  and doesn't go to church (7 min. 27 sec.).
- As soon as difficulties arise, goes to see the Comte
  and confronts him (31 min. 49 sec.).
- Makes a point of buying jewellery from Roux the
  river rat when she knows the Comte is watching (53
  min. 08 sec.).
- Organises Armande's party.
- Organises the Easter festival.

Week Four:
Getting Real –
The Power of Acceptance

Show video
In: Vianne and Anouk in bed, just *after* 'You make the most wonderful chocolate.'   35 min. 08 sec.
Out: Just after Vianne: 'Goodnight, mama.' 38 min. 45 sec.

1. See sequence 12 min. 10 sec. onwards for example of Vianne's 'air of mystery' sales technique.

2. 'Pagan' – *Chambers Dictionary* defines it as 'one who is not a Christian, Jew or Muslim. More recently, one who has no religion, one who sets a high value on sensual pleasures'.

4, 5 & 6. Note that I have said 'different brands of Christianity' and 'different churches'. People within your group are likely to have come across a wide range of experiences, as will people trying to find out about the Christian faith. Try and keep the questions broad to reflect them all.

Show video
In: Boats going up river, Anouk watching, just *after* children playing on banks and child calls, 'Hey, look'.

50 min. 08 sec.

Out: Just after Comte says in village meeting, ' . . . but we can help them to understand they are not welcome.'

56 min. 27 sec.

8. 'Helping someone understand they are not welcome' may be necessary in a wide range of situations: you may have had to deal with an employee who is lazy or unsuitable, a tenant who is impossible to live with, a friend or classmate of your own child who is disrespectful or unruly. It may be necessary in a church service if someone becomes disruptive, or

even in a Lent group if someone is so difficult or dominant that it ruins the whole group.

10. If people in your group have experience of any organisational 'mission' situations, then it might be worth discussing what safeguards need to be put in place within that organisation to ensure that the sharing of faith is done appropriately, e.g. training sessions, not one-to-one with the opposite sex, the appropriateness of evangelising children, whether aid should be given unconditionally or with evangelical strings attached, etc.

NB: This session may have touched on all sorts of issues regarding different beliefs or practices. Make a note of anything that is a particular issue within the group and follow it up if possible by offering appropriate reading matter, or follow-up sessions to explore the issue concerned. See p. 91, References and Resources, for some recommended reading on other faiths and New Age beliefs.

Week Five:
Growing Up – The Process of Change

Show video
In: Caroline in yard with bike, just *after* Roux says goodbye to Vianne, 'I know. I'm sorry. I'm sorry.'

1 hr 29 min. 45 sec.

Out: Just after Caroline says, 'Goodnight, Paul.'

1 hr 34 min. 14 sec.

Brainstorm questions 1–4
You will probably find it easiest to go through these

questions person by person. Below is a list of the main characters and their stages of growth.

Caroline

1. Needs to acknowledge that her fear of loss is making her overprotective towards her son.
2. Seeing Luc enjoying himself dancing on the boat becomes a catalyst for change.
3. She demonstrates change by doing up the bike for him to ride, and by challenging the Comte about his wife's absence.
4. She needs to shake off the Comte's control.

Luc

1. Needs to acknowledge his own worth, and the fact that he is a person in his own right.
2. Meeting his grandmother becomes a point of change.
3. He demonstrates change by continuing to see his grandmother secretly, and by going to her party.
4. He needs to shake off his mother's tight protectiveness.

Josephine

1. Acknowledges to Vianne her stealing and the fact that she is being beaten.
2. Vianne actively seeking her out and expressing her acceptance becomes a catalyst for change.
3. She takes action by leaving her drunken husband Serge.
4. She needs to step out from under Serge's control.

Comte

1. Needs to acknowledge the dangers of his control over others; that his wife isn't coming back; his own

weakness. Before the cross he says, 'All my efforts have been for nothing' (1 hr 41 min. 10 sec.).

2. Change begins when he sees that Serge set the boats on fire, in response to what he thought the Comte wanted, and when he tastes the chocolate.
3. He shows his change by attending Vianne's Festival.
4. He probably needs to shake off the expectations that have been put on him by his ancestry.

Père Henri

1. Needs to acknowledge that the Comte's control is inappropriate and that he needs to assert his own ideas.
2. Change probably only begins when he finds the Comte in the chocolaterie and he seizes his opportunity to gain the upper hand. You can see it beginning to assert itself during Armande's funeral, where he is clearly unhappy with what he has been given to say.
3. He demonstrates change by preaching a sermon from his own heart.
4. He shakes off the Comte's control.

Vianne

1. Has to acknowledge, to Roux the river rat, that Anouk actually hates travelling from town to town (1 hr 22 min. 30 sec.). Perhaps has to acknowledge, following Josephine's insistence, that her moving on is not just in response to the wind, but could also be running away.
2. The point at which she spills the ashes and then discovers the people in the kitchen preparing for the festival becomes the point at which she changes (1 hr 37 min. 38 sec.).

3. She demonstrates change by throwing her mother's ashes to the winds.
4. She has to shake off her mother's controlling influence.

There is also change in other minor characters:

- Guillaume Blerot, the elderly gentleman with Charlie the dog, and the Widow Audel
- the Marceaux, the couple whose sex life is reawakened
- possibly Roux in that he returns at the end of the film
- possibly Anouk in that she begins to resist her mother's demands to move on.

However, these do not demonstrate the process of change in the same way, and are probably not worth pursuing.

5. The main point I am expecting to draw from these is that people generally feel more sympathy towards people who admit their weaknesses, like Princess Diana, than those who continue to deny and hide them, like Jeffrey Archer. However, the questions are bound to provoke a mixed response and that is fine. Although the first two examples probably need no introduction, the following notes will refresh your memory about the other two individuals.

Jonathan Aitken was a Conservative Cabinet Minister when he was accused of pimping, arms dealing and corruption in 1995. His subsequent libel action against *The Guardian* failed and led to him being tried and found guilty of perjury on the issue of a hotel bill paid for by Mohammed al Fayed. He has since become a Christian and gone on to attend theological college. His autobiography, *Pride and Perjury* (HarperCollins, 2000), is an interesting study in the process of growth and change.

Michael Barrymore's popularity as an entertainer was not seriously dented by his coming out as gay, nor by his acknowledgement of his drink and drugs problems. However, the discovery in 2000 that a young man, virtually unknown to Barrymore, had drowned in his swimming pool during a drugs-fuelled party, brought out further damaging revelations. In an interview with Martin Bashir in 2001, Barrymore, whilst denying any direct involvement in the man's death, admitted his own weaknesses and feelings of guilt.

6. Although I am anticipating that relationships will often have been strengthened by revelations of weakness, there may well be very mixed reactions and responses to this question. It is important to allow space for these mixed responses. The admission of weaknesses is a complex affair, both for those who admit them and for those who listen.

Show video
In: In church, just after Comte is found in shop window, 'I'll think of something.'   1 hr 45 min. 40 sec.
Out: After Vianne throws ashes: 'the north wind got weary and went on its way.'   1 hr 50 min. 07 sec.

7. Again, many people's experience is that they have been strengthened by weakness or failure, but there may well be very mixed responses to this question. Allow them space and look out for any responses that may need follow-up prayer or counselling.

9. The images I had in mind were the twirling woman in white with 'wings', who could evoke ideas of an angel or of a white dove, and the man blowing fire. Another, of course, is the recurring image of the wind. All of these are symbols of the Holy Spirit for Christians, and it is perhaps worth touching briefly on the idea that not only does the Holy Spirit often stir up change in us, but is also available to us to

help us through that process of change. In the film, the images are, of course, not used in any Christian sense. They are, however, not there by accident, but as a way of expressing the release of the human spirit.

10. One aspect that might shed light on this discussion is the songs you sing in your worship. Ask yourself how these relate to the Jesus of the Gospels. In our trial group discussions, people identified various types of songs which they felt did not quite square with Jesus, the actual man we read about:
    - the 'soppy': 'I'll sing a love song to Jesus', 'Gentle Jesus meek and mild'
    - the warlike: 'In heavenly armour, we'll conquer the land', 'Battle hymn of the Republic'
    - the idealistic: 'I wanna see Jesus lifted high, a banner that flies across this land . . .'

However, be aware that people react very differently. Each of these was also someone else's favourite!

NB: In conclusion – it might be good to ask at the end of the course whether there are any unresolved questions or issues any group members feel they want to take further. Again, offer an opportunity to pray over or discuss anything the course has brought up.

The Curious History of Chocolate

It is fascinating to see how the story of *Chocolat* has its roots in the real-life history of chocolate. As always, truth is stranger than fiction.

Chocolate and ritual

For native South Americans, chocolate has always had religious and ritualistic significance. Even today, one of the remnant Maya tribes still prepares two kinds of chocolate drinks, one for their own consumption and one for offering to the gods. The production of chocolate (or cacao, as it should more properly be called in its original form) began with the Maya, although when the Spanish discovered the New World, it was the use of cacao by the Aztecs that was documented. At that time the beans were used as currency, a custom that continued among poorer people right up until 150 years ago. According to sixteenth-century writings, a slave was worth 100 cacao beans, while a rabbit or the services of a prostitute was worth around ten.

Chocolate was frequently used in Aztec and Maya rituals and banquets. It was mixed into a liquid used to 'baptise' young boys and girls, and the cacao pods were given as offerings to the gods. (Not for nothing was the cacao plant classified with the Latin name *Theobroma Cacao* – 'the food of the gods'.) Chocolate drinks also had a role in marriage and betrothal ceremonies, much like today's champagne. The Aztecs believed that cacao was of divine origin and that drinking chocolate gave mortals some of the god Quetzalcoatl's wisdom. In Aztec society it was seen very much as a drink for the upper echelons of society – lords and nobility, rich merchants and warriors.

Chocolate and class structure

When chocolate reached Europe, this practice of chocolate as a drink for the upper classes continued. It arrived during the Renaissance but it was in the Baroque age that its popularity spread, radiating out from Spain to Italy and, of course, France, where over the centuries prominent chocolate enthusiasts included Cardinal Richelieu, Louis XIV, Voltaire and the Marquis de Sade. The drinking of chocolate (and drinking it was, for chocolate as confectionery did not appear until the early nineteenth century) was a ritualistic part of aristocratic life, with the whipping up of foam by means of a wooden swizzle stick called a *molinillo* all part of the tradition.

In the Catholic lands of France, Spain and Italy, included in these top ranks of society were the clergy. Jesuits particularly became partial to chocolate, even becoming traders themselves.

Chocolate never quite caught on in the same way in Protestant England, arriving along with tea and coffee in the 1650s, when Cromwell's puritanical rule discouraged such luxuries. It never gained quite as much popularity as its competitors and was never such an upper class prerogative. Indeed, it was said that chocolate was southern, Catholic and aristocratic, while coffee was northern, Protestant and middle class.

Chocolate and the Church

Chocolate and Catholicism, however, have often had an uneasy relationship.

The question of whether chocolate broke an ecclesiastical fast was a perennial one. Drinks were allowed, but did chocolate merely quench the thirst or did it provide sustenance as well? The arguments raged for two and half centuries, and at least seven popes made pronouncements on it, all agreeing that it did *not* break the Lenten fast.

Nevertheless more puritanical priests continued to stir up the debate, occasionally bringing in the equally perennial argument of chocolate as an aphrodisiac, 'exciting the venereal appetite'. However, reports that a young Peruvian saint, St Rose of Lima, was presented with a cup of chocolate by an angel after a particularly taxing session of prayer and visions, did wonders for the pro-chocolate lobby.

Even so, in 1650 the Society of Jesus in the New World issued an act prohibiting Jesuits from drinking chocolate. Embarrassingly, they were forced to rescind it when many of their students started leaving because of the ban.

The story of *Chocolat* is not the first instance of feisty women coming up against the religious establishment. In the seventeenth century in the South American colonial city of Chiapa Real, the upper class Spanish ladies claimed to suffer from such weak stomachs that they could not get through a service in the cathedral without taking a cup of hot chocolate. Their Indian maids would bustle in during the Mass or the sermon to serve them, so exasperating the bishop that he threatened to excommunicate anyone who ate or drank during divine service. In protest, the ladies withdrew to attend Mass at the local convent.

After presiding over his now deserted cathedral, the bishop one day took a cup of chocolate himself and soon afterwards became ill and died. Now, down the ages chocolate has always had a reputation as a favourite vehicle for poison, being particularly effective at disguising it. This unfortunate bishop had apparently suffered the fate of being poisoned by one of his disgruntled flock.

Chocolate and the march of 'progress'

As the demand for chocolate grew in Europe, so its production changed. Thus it was that cacao groves were planted in the West Indies and the hulls of the three-way trade ships began to be filled with slaves from Africa to labour at their harvesting. Still chocolate was used mainly as a drink, and just occasionally as a flavouring for food.

But in 1828 a Dutch chemist named Van Houten discovered a process for manufacturing powdered chocolate with a low fat content. 'Cocoa' had been born. The progression to the modern-day chocolate bar was continued by an English Quaker dynasty, the Fry family of Bristol, who found a way to mix this cocoa powder with other ingredients to a form in which chocolate could be moulded. Their rivals, Cadburys in Birmingham and Rowntrees in York, both also Quakers, were quick to take up the challenge and the great British consumption of chocolate began. At least these Quaker firms had a social conscience, with Cadburys and Rowntrees building model towns, most notably Bourneville, for their workers, and Frys fighting for improved conditions of plantation workers.

The next leap forward in chocolate production was with the Swiss, when Henri Nestlé created milk chocolate in 1867. When Milton Hershey started his chocolate empire in Pennsylvania in 1893 the commercial potential of chocolate knew no bounds.

Of course, as chocolate gradually became big business, so it also bore less and less resemblance to its original form, with sugar, vegetable fats and milk powder often far outweighing the actual cacao content. Today's chocoholics could in fact be sugar addicts.

Chocolate – good or bad for you?

Throughout its long history, opinions have been divided as to whether or not eating chocolate is good for you. Even back in Baroque times, it was claimed on one hand to promote nervousness and on the other to aid digestion.

Present-day scientific opinion varies just as wildly. On the minus side, chocolate, like its early competitors tea and coffee, contains alkaloids – in the case of chocolate: caffeine and theobromine. These alkaloids stimulate the central nervous system and are therefore claimed to cause tension and insomnia. Caffeine, much the stronger of these two alkaloids, is known to be addictive, producing withdrawal symptoms of extreme headache. However, cocoa contains much less caffeine than coffee or even tea.

On the plus side, some doctors claim it to be an anti-depressant, interacting with female hormones to produce incredible pre-menstrual cravings for chocolate. A survey by French doctor Hervé Robert, published in 1990, found that the caffeine, theobromine, serotonin and phenylethyl-amine contained in chocolate make it a tonic and an anti-stress agent, enhancing pleasurable activities including making love.

This is an area in which the reputation of chocolate has been strangely consistent. It has been claimed to be an aphrodisiac right down the centuries from the Aztec empire to *Chocolat* the movie. In 1662 a Dr Stubbe reported that, 'The mighty lover Casanova found the drink as useful a lubrication to seduction as champagne.' Whether there is any evidence for this, or any other of chocolate's claimed physical effects, will no doubt continue to be researched and debated. But on the grounds of 'a little of what you fancy does you good', chocolate looks here to stay.

The Unfair Economics of Chocolate

In the last few years, there have been several shock exposés claiming near slavery conditions of those who work at the supply end of the cocoa industry.

These have eventually provoked action and on 1 October 2001 a Protocol was signed in which the US cocoa and chocolate industry agreed to eliminate child slavery from the chocolate industry. It also 'recognised as a matter of urgency, the need to end slavery, serfdom and debt bondage in the growing and processing of West African cocoa beans'.

The truth is, however, that no one really has clear evidence of how prevalent these types of labour exploitation are. The first large-scale survey is now being undertaken by the International Institute for Tropical Agriculture, surveying 3000 farms across West Africa.

'Child slavery' in the cocoa industry has hit the headlines and it certainly does exist, but probably no more so than in other third world industries, as the production of cocoa tends to demand strength and skills that children do not have.

Moreover, 90 per cent of the chocolate we eat is not grown on huge plantations but on smallholdings – family farms or village co-operatives, where preventing children taking part could have an adverse effect rather than a positive one.

The most oppressive slavery frequently occurs in the form of bonded labour where someone, on being obliged to take out a loan for a basic necessity such as medicine for a child, is then forced into working for the supplier of the loan, often long hours for seven days a week with only basic food and shelter as payment. Sometimes the loan can never be repaid and is passed from generation to generation. Several sharp drops in the cocoa market in recent years have had this end result on many farmers.

Ultimately, it is this that is the real issue: the price paid for cocoa.

Even with fairly traded chocolate such as Maya Gold, the cocoa farmer only gets around 3.9 per cent of the price of a bar, with the supermarket getting 34.1 per cent, the overheads of production and other ingredients eating up 36.8 per cent, the trading company getting 10.4 per cent and the government 14.8 per cent in VAT.

And this is in a chocolate bar that actually contains a significant amount of cocoa – 55 per cent as opposed to the 20 per cent of most popular chocolate bars. From a typical milk chocolate bar from one of the giant companies, a Ghanaian farmer can expect to see just 0.5p from a 90p chocolate bar.

So if you want to make a difference to the lives of at least some of the 14 million people involved in the cocoa industry, then make sure that when you do buy chocolate you get one of the growing number of fair trade chocolate products now available.

Some of the most easily available are Divine and Dubble, produced by the Day Chocolate Company. Launched with support from The Body Shop, Christian Aid and Comic Relief, Day is unique in that the farmers that grow the cocoa are also shareholders in the company. The farmers' organisation, called *Kuapa Kokoo* in Ghanaian, operates a credit union and buys agricultural tools at bulk purchasing rates, passing savings on to the farmers. Village co-operatives that perform particularly well are awarded prizes such as machetes or gum boots for use by the whole community. More importantly the scheme gives the farmers a chance to have a say in how the chocolate is produced and sold, as well as a share of the profits.

Imagine if all the people doing this course decided to purchase fair trade chocolate – and made a point of letting their local supermarket know they would like to buy it, if it is not readily available. Yes, our purchasing power is just a drop in the ocean compared to the might of Nestlé or Cadbury's. But the story of *Chocolat* demonstrates that, even when the existing power structures seem unshakeable, just one person who sticks to their guns *can* make a difference.

Chocolate products fairly traded and available in the UK

Divine Milk Chocolate, Darkly Divine Plain Chocolate and Dubble bars – *available from several supermarket chains*

Green and Black Milk Chocolate and Maya Gold Plain – *available from Sainsbury's and health food shops*

Oxfam Masca Organic: cappucino, milk, orange and plain (all organic) – *from Oxfam shops or www.oxfam.org.uk/ fair_trade.hmtl*

Traidcraft: milk, plain, cappucino and praline – *from fair trade sources or www.traidcraft.co.uk, tel: 0191 491 05910.*

Also available are:

    Equal Exchange organic cocoa
    Green and Black organic cocoa
    Oxfam African cocoa

You can buy fair trade products online from a site run by Oxfam and Traidcraft: www.fairtradeonline.com

More information on labour abuses can be found on the web site of Anti-Slavery International: www.antislavery.org.

A good source of information on the chocolate industry worldwide can be found on the website of New Internationalist magazine, where one of their back numbers is dedicated to the subject:

www.oneworld.org/niissue304Aug98

Ideas for a Chocolate Feast

When our initial group did this, we invited everyone to come wearing something to represent their favourite chocolate – either brand name or flavour, and cryptic clues welcome. Guessing everyone's favourites then proved an enjoyable ice-breaker. You could have dancing or party games after the feast, but we found people were quite happy just to chat.

Suggested menu

Starter
Fresh fruit with Semi-sweet Chocolate Ganache

Main course
Mole Poblano – spicy chicken with chocolate
or
Beef with Balsamic Vinegar and Chocolate

Served with plain rice and mixed vegetables

Pudding
(Recipes for chocolate desserts are legion, but the following has a sharp taste which complements the chocolate)
Pineapple and Chocolate Cheesecake

Recipes

Semi-sweet Chocolate Ganache (Serves 12 generously)
8 fl oz /240 ml double cream
1 oz /28 g unsalted butter
1 oz /28 g caster sugar
12 oz/ 340 g plain chocolate

Heat the double cream, butter and sugar in a large saucepan over medium high heat, stirring regularly. Bring the mixture gently to a boil.

Break the chocolate into 1 in. squares and place in a heatproof bowl, pour the boiling cream mixture over it and allow to stand for 5 minutes. Stir until smooth. Allow to cool for another 10 minutes and serve when it is still slightly warm and not too solid.

Serve with a platter of fresh fruit: grapes, sliced apple, banana, orange, kiwi fruit, melon, strawberries, etc.

Mole Poblano (Serves 12)
A festive dish from Mexico, traditionally made with turkey, but adapted here with chicken.

3 large onions
6 cloves garlic
4 tbsp. cooking oil
3 red peppers
3 lb/1360 g boneless chicken breast or stir-fry chicken
8 oz/227 g raisins
3 x 14 oz/400 g tin chopped tomatoes
2 slices white bread
8 oz/227 g chopped nuts
6 oz/170 g sesame seeds
½ tsp. star anise
3 tsp. chilli pepper (or to taste)
½ tsp. ground allspice
½ tsp. ground coriander
2 chicken stock cubes

6 oz/170 g dark bitter chocolate
Salt and freshly ground black pepper
Fresh coriander or parsley to garnish

Peel and chop the onions and garlic. Trim, de-seed and chop the peppers. Tear the bread into small pieces.

Cut the chicken into 1 in. cubes, and fry in 2 tbsp. oil until brown. Drain and remove into casserole.

While the chicken is cooking, put the onion, garlic, peppers, raisins, tomatoes and bread into a food processor and blend to a paste. Add the chopped nuts, 4 oz/113 g sesame seeds and spices and sauté the paste in the remainder of the oil for about 5 minutes. Transfer to the casserole.

Make the chicken stock cubes up to 1.5 pints and add this to the pan, together with the chocolate broken into small pieces. Bring gently to the boil until the chocolate has melted, then add to the casserole and stir thoroughly. Check for seasoning and add salt and pepper as needed.

Put the covered casserole in a moderate oven Gas 5, 200° C and cook for half an hour.

To serve, sprinkle with chopped coriander or parsley and the remaining sesame seeds lightly toasted.

Beef with Balsamic Vinegar and Chocolate (Serves 12)
3 medium onions, finely chopped
6 cloves garlic, finely chopped
2 tbsp. olive oil
2 tbsp. butter
3 lb/1360 g stewing beef
4 tbsp. balsamic vinegar
2 x 14 oz/400g tin chopped tomatoes
3 tbsp. tomato puree
3 oz/85 g dark bitter chocolate
1½ tsp. dried thyme
½ tsp. dried marjoram
salt and freshly ground black pepper

Preheat oven to 325°F/170°C/150°C Fan/Gas mark 3.

Fry the onions and garlic gently in the oil and butter and transfer to a casserole dish when done. Meanwhile cut the beef into 4 cm/1½ in. squares and then fry until browned and transfer to the casserole dish.

Add the vinegar to the pan and boil briefly, scraping the sediment from the bottom. Then add chopped tomatoes and tomato puree.

Season well, add the chocolate broken into small pieces, the herbs and about half a cup of water. Stir until the chocolate is melted, then transfer to the casserole.

Add enough water to come just to the top of the meat. Cook in the oven for one and a half to two hours until the meat is tender. A stir halfway through is of great benefit.

Pineapple and Chocolate Cheesecake
(12 smallish portions)
3 oz/85 g butter or margarine
1 packet (400 g) plain chocolate digestive biscuits (although you probably only need about two thirds of the packet)
1 tin crushed pineapple
1 packet lemon jelly
2 oz/56 g caster sugar
1 (500 g) carton fromage frais
1 small tin pineapple rings (to decorate)
Dark glacé cherries (to decorate)
About 2 oz/56 g dark chocolate (to decorate)

Put the butter in a large bowl and heat gently in the microwave until melted. Put the chocolate biscuits on a tray and crush with a rolling pin. Add the crushed biscuits to the melted butter and stir until thoroughly mixed. Press the biscuit mixture into the base and sides of a 12 in./30 cm flan dish.

Put the crushed pineapple into a sieve over a bowl to

drain the excess liquid. Put the whole jelly into a jug and melt in the microwave for one minute. Add about 3 fl oz/90 ml of the juice from the crushed pineapple. (Alternatively, divide into cubes and melt with a small amount of pineapple juice in a saucepan).

Into a large mixing bowl, put the fromage frais, the drained crushed pineapple and the jelly mixture. Stir thoroughly and add caster sugar to taste if needed.

Put the fromage frais mixture into the biscuit flan base and store in the fridge until set.

When set, decorate with half rings of pineapple and cherries round the edge and grated chocolate in the centre.

References and Resources

Introduction
Definition of community from Community Building in Britain, an organisation which offers workshops based on the writings of Dr M. Scott Peck. Scott Peck, a psychiatrist whose spiritual exploration has led him to become a Christian, is well worth reading. His titles include:

On personal growth and relationships: *The Road Less Travelled* (Hutchinson & Co., 1983)

On journeying into faith: *Further Along the Road Less Travelled* (Simon & Schuster, 1993)

On creating true community: *A Different Drum* (Rider, 1987)

Week Two
Antoine de Saint-Exupéry, *The Little Prince* (Pan 1975, first published 1945)

Graham Kendrick & Steve Thompson, 'Teach me to dance' (Make Way Music, 1993)

Week Three
Edward Bond, *Plays One* (Methuen, 1962): the quotation is from the author's note on 'Saved'.

Week Four
John Drane, *What is the New Age Saying to the Church?* (Marshall Pickering, 1991)

Postscript

Gerard W. Hughes, *Oh God, Why?* (Bible Reading Fellowship, 1993)

Also by Gerard W. Hughes:

On his own pilgrimages: *In Search of a Way* (DLT, 1986)

On exploring your own spiritual journey: *God of Surprises* (DLT, 1985)

The Curious History of Chocolate

Information taken from:

Sophie D. and Michael D. Coe, *The True History of Chocolate* (Thames & Hudson, 1996)

Ideas for a Chocolate Feast

Semi-sweet Chocolate Ganache adapted from: Marcel Desaulniers, *Death by Chocolate – the last word on a consuming passion* (Virgin Books, 1992)

Mole Poblano adapted from: Michael Barry, *Chocolate the crafty way* (Jarrold Publishing, 1998) and from *The True History of Chocolate*

Beef with Balsamic Vinegar and Chocolate adapted from: Michael Barry, *Chocolate the crafty way* (Jarrold Publishing, 1998)

And, of course, most importantly:

Chocolat, Miramax 2000, directed by Lasse Hallström, and starring Juliette Binoche, Judi Dench, Alfred Molina, Lena Olin and Johnny Depp; screenplay by Robert Nelson Jacobs. Based on the novel, *Chocolat* by Joanne Harris (Black Swan, 1999)